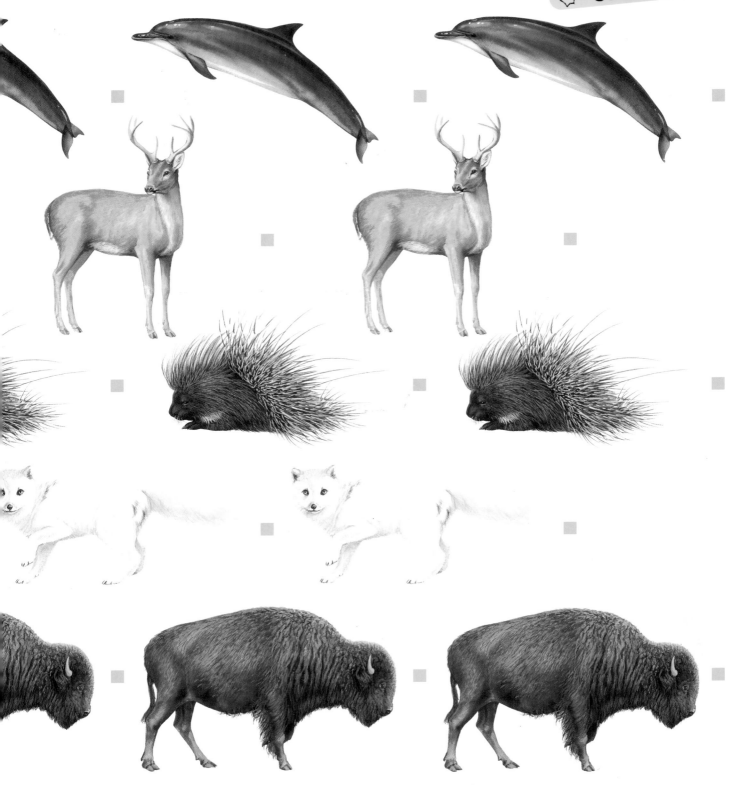

Poison Ivy and Poison Oak

This weed (above) gives you an itchy rash. Poison Ivy grows like a vine, and Poison Oak like a shrub. Try to remember what the leaves look like, and do not touch it. If you do touch it, washing your hands as soon as possible may reduce the itching. Your local drug store will also have various remedies.

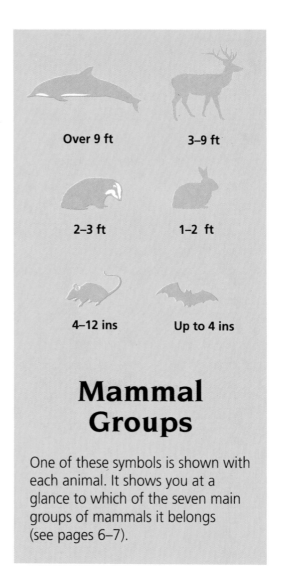

Over 9 ft   3–9 ft

2–3 ft   1–2 ft

4–12 ins   Up to 4 ins

Mammal Groups

One of these symbols is shown with each animal. It shows you at a glance to which of the seven main groups of mammals it belongs (see pages 6–7).

MAMMALS
OF NORTH AMERICA

John Burton

ILLUSTRATIONS BY
Jim Channell

EDITED BY
Angela Royston

THUNDER BAY
P·R·E·S·S

Conservation

Every animal is closely linked to its surroundings. It feeds on other animals or plants and it makes its nest or den in trees, among rocks or bushes, or under the ground. Many animals prefer particular kinds of climate and landscape. As you learn more about a habitat, you will get to know which plants and animals you can expect to find there.

Hundreds of years ago, many more wild animals used to live in North America, but many of their habitats have been damaged or destroyed by agriculture, industry, and the pollution that both of these cause. Some wild animals are in danger of disappearing altogether. These animals are often protected by federal law, or by state laws.

On page 78 you will find the names of some organizations who campaign for the protection of particular animals and habitats. By joining them and supporting their efforts, you can help to preserve our animals and their habitats.

Countryside Code

1 **Always go collecting with a friend,** and always tell an adult where you have gone.
2 **Leave any wild animals that you find alone**—they may attack you if frightened.
3 **Leave their nests or dens untouched**.
4 **Keep your dog on a leash**.
5 **Ask permission** before exploring or crossing private property.
6 **Keep to footpaths** as much as possible.
7 **Leave fence gates as you find them.**
8 **Wear long pants, shoes, and a long-sleeved shirt** in deer tick country.
9 **Ask your parents not to light fires** except in fireplaces in special picnic areas.

Thunder Bay Press
5880 Oberlin Drive
Suite 400
San Diego, CA 92121

First published in the United States
by Thunder Bay Press, 1995

© Dragon's World, 1995
© Text Dragon's World, 1995
© Species illustrations Jim Channell,
  1991 & 1995
© Other illustrations Dragon's World, 1995

Simplified text and captions by Angela Royston, based on *Mammals of North America* by John Burton.

Habitat paintings by Tim Hayward.
Headbands by Antonia Phillips.
Identification and activities illustrations by Mr Gay Galsworthy.

Editor   Diana Briscoe
Designer   James Lawrence
Design Assistants Karen Ferguson
                  Victoria Furbisher
Art Director   John Strange
Editorial Director Pippa Rubinstein

Library of Congress Cataloging in Publication Data
Royston. Angela.
    Mammals / Angela Royston.
        p.   ca. — (Science Nature Guides)
        Includes bibliographical references (p.78)
    and index.
        ISBN 1–57145–016–5 : $12.95
        1. Mammals—North America—Juvenile literature.
        2. Mammals—North America—Identification—
        Juvenile literature. [1. Mammals.]
I. Title   II. Series
QL715.R66   1995
599.097—dc20
                                        94–27458
                                             CIP
                                             AC

Printed in Italy

Contents

What Is a Mammal?.........4–5
What To Look For....................6–7

**Found
In Many Habitats**.............8–19
Encouraging Bats 20–21

Woods & Forests...........22–29
Signs of Mammals.................30–31

**Grasslands
& Savanna** 32–41
Hunting for Hunters.............42–43

Deserts...........................44–47
Tracking Deer........................48–49

Mountains & Tundra.....50–59

Rivers & Waterways......60–63
Detecting Rodents................64–65

Coasts & Marine...........66–77

Find Out Some More..................78
Index & Glossary...................79–81

What Is a Mammal?

Mammals are the most recent development of the animal kingdom. They include the species (groupings) of animals that are closest to humans in behavior and intelligence. Almost all of them have warm blood and give birth to live young who drink their mother's milk. There are mammals everywhere, in the air and sea, as well as on and under the ground, but most like to stay out of sight.

This book will help you to become more familiar with mammals. It tells you where you are likely to see them and how to recognize them. It tells you what signs and tracks they leave behind. Some of the animals in this book are very common and are often seen, like squirrels in city parks or jack rabbits in the countryside. But you will probably only see grizzly bears or beavers in a wildlife park or nature reserve. This book groups the animals according to the habitat, or type of countryside, in which they are most common in the wild.

The life of a mammal

Most mammals develop inside their mothers and are born fully formed. The mother feeds them with her own milk. They rely on their mothers, and sometimes their fathers too, to look after them until they are strong enough to fend for themselves. Lions, foxes, and other meat-eaters teach their young to hunt. Small mammals, like mice, have several litters each year. The young stay with the mother for only a few weeks before they are ready to leave home.

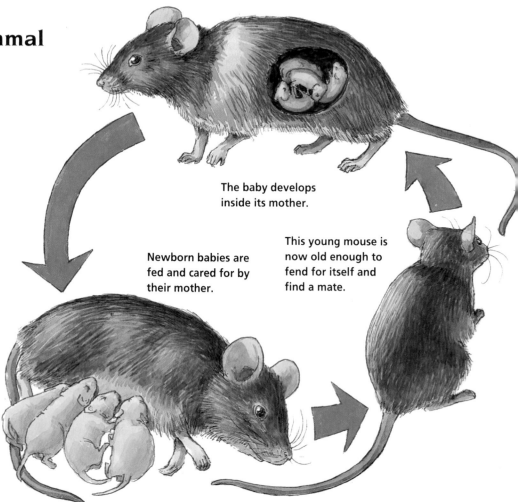

The baby develops inside its mother.

Newborn babies are fed and cared for by their mother.

This young mouse is now old enough to fend for itself and find a mate.

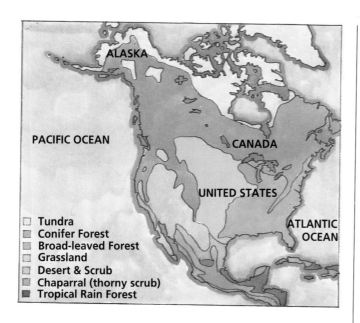

- ☐ Tundra
- ☐ Conifer Forest
- ☐ Broad-leaved Forest
- ☐ Grassland
- ☐ Desert & Scrub
- ☐ Chaparral (thorny scrub)
- ■ Tropical Rain Forest

Habitat Picture Bands

Each habitat has a different picture band at the top of the page. These are shown below.

Found In Many Habitats

Woods & Forests

Grasslands & Savanna

Deserts

Mountains & Tundra

Rivers & Waterways

Coasts & Marine

How to use this book

To identify a mammal you do not recognize, such as the mammals shown here, follow these steps.

1 **As you will probably only get a brief look at a mammal in the wild**, note down the things you noticed about it in your field notebook (see page 31) before trying to identify the animal. Was it big or small? Did it have a long tail? Can you find its tracks to give you additional clues?

2 **Work out which habitat you are in.** There is a description at the start of each section which will help. Each habitat has a different picture band, as shown below left.

3 **Which of the six main groups of mammals does it belong to?** Look at pages 6–7 to see the main differences between bats, insectivores, rodents, carnivores, ungulates, seals, and whales and dolphins. Mammals from the same group are shown together in each habitat. The rodent shown below is a house mouse (see page 19.)

4 **If you can't find the mammal in the first habitat you check,** then look through other habitats. Most mammals are found in more than one kind of habitat. You will find the carnivore shown below (a red fox) on page 13.

5 **If you still can't find the mammal,** you may have to look in a larger field guide (see page 79 for some suggestions.) You may have spotted a very rare mammal!

What To Look For

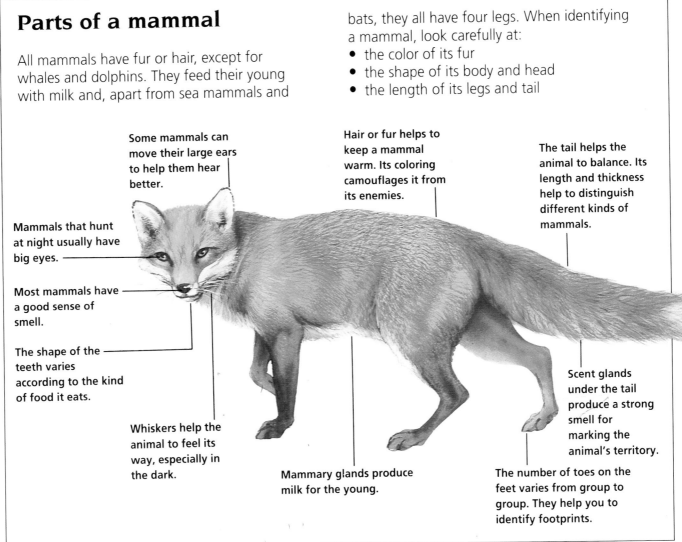

Parts of a mammal

All mammals have fur or hair, except for whales and dolphins. They feed their young with milk and, apart from sea mammals and bats, they all have four legs. When identifying a mammal, look carefully at:

- the color of its fur
- the shape of its body and head
- the length of its legs and tail

Some mammals can move their large ears to help them hear better.

Hair or fur helps to keep a mammal warm. Its coloring camouflages it from its enemies.

The tail helps the animal to balance. Its length and thickness help to distinguish different kinds of mammals.

Mammals that hunt at night usually have big eyes.

Most mammals have a good sense of smell.

The shape of the teeth varies according to the kind of food it eats.

Whiskers help the animal to feel its way, especially in the dark.

Mammary glands produce milk for the young.

Scent glands under the tail produce a strong smell for marking the animal's territory.

The number of toes on the feet varies from group to group. They help you to identify footprints.

Mammals are divided into several main groups. They have much the same bones in their bodies, but their length and shape vary according to their lifestyle.

Bats

Bats are the only mammals that can fly. Their wings are made of skin stretched between their long finger bones and back legs. Their skulls are similar to those of insectivores (see page 7,) but are much smaller.

Carnivores

These meat-eaters include lions, foxes, weasels, and bears. Most carnivores have long, sleek bodies and long, strong legs for chasing and pouncing on their prey. They have strong jaws with many sharp teeth for tearing.

Seals

Seals have large, streamlined, hairy bodies and short front legs modified into paddles, but their back limbs are flippers. They can swim under water, but surface to breathe air. They feed at sea, but come ashore to give birth.

Insectivores

They include armadillos, moles, and shrews. They all have poor eyesight, but front feet which are good for digging into the soil. They have small heads and long jaws.

Whales & Dolphins

This group has no back limbs and only short front flippers. Their young are born at sea. All must come to the surface to breathe air. Some whales have teeth, others have "baleen plates" through which they sift the water for tiny shrimps and plankton.

Ungulates

Deer, sheep, goats, and cattle come into this group. They all have hooves—these are actually modified fingernails. They have several stomach compartments so they can digest tough plants. They often bring partly digested food back into their mouths to chew again—this is called chewing the cud. Instead of sharp, upper teeth they have a horny pad for chewing leaves and grass. Many ungulates also have horns or antlers.

Rodents

These include mice, rats, gophers, and woodchucks. They have large front teeth for gnawing. Rabbits and hares are closely related to this group.

Found In Many Habitats

There are some mammals that can live almost anywhere. The animals in this section are so adaptable you will find them in many of the other habitats as well. Many thrive near people, so look for signs of them in suburban yards, parks, public gardens, and vacant lots.

People have created buildings, yards, parks, and golf courses for their own purposes, not realizing that to animals they resemble natural habitats. Buildings are like rocky cliffs with holes and cracks. Bats can roost in cellars and attics; foxes make their dens under yard sheds, raccoons in chimney flues. Both will feed from garbage cans.

A golf course is much like a clearing in a wood, a well-grazed meadow, or a prairie. Look for signs of deer, moles, rabbits, and skunks here. There are not usually many big trees in suburban areas, but woodland mammals such as flying squirrels, bats, and mice will nest in bird and bat boxes instead.

Although your home may be surrounded by mammals, they may not be easy to see. You might have to get up in the very early morning to see them. Unfortunately, one of the best ways of seeing wild mammals is to look for their bodies on the roadside.

Many wild animals carry disease, so **don't** touch them. The picture shows eight mammals from this book. How many can you recognize?

Badger, Big Brown Bat, Eastern Chipmunk, White-tailed Deer, Cottontail Rabbits, Raccoon, Short-tailed Weasel, Woodchuck.

Found in Many Habitats

Bats come out at dusk, and are almost impossible to identify as they flit about in the dark. Do not confuse them with birds—they come out after most birds have gone to roost. Bats are the only mammals that can fly. Their wings are formed by thin skin which stretches between the very long fingers of their front legs and across to their ankles. If you do get a chance to see one clearly, look at its ears to help you identify it. In particular, look for the large lobe of skin that guards the entrance to its ears—it is called the "tragus" and is much more noticeable than in humans. For more about bats, see the activities on page 20.

Little Brown Myotis

The Little Brown Myotis is one of the commonest bats in North America, and is found almost everywhere, except in southern and southeastern states. Its fur is brown above and buff below, and its ears are quite long and have a short, rounded tragus. It feeds on flying insects near water or forests, and roosts in buildings near water. The females gather in large colonies (groups) to give birth to their young. In fall, northern bats fly south (migrate) to sleep (hibernate) in caves, mines, and other tunnels.

Bat
Length: 3–3½ ins, of which tail is about 1½ ins
Feeds on insects
Young: usually one baby, very rarely twins

Eastern Pipistrelle

As its name suggests, this bat is found only in eastern North America. It is the smallest eastern bat, and its tragus is shorter and blunter than that of other small bats. Its fur is yellowish to drab brown. During the summer it roosts mostly in trees, and emerges in early evening to look for food. It flies slowly, constantly changing direction. In winter, it may fly south or sleep in caves and mines.

Bat
Length: 3 ins, of which tail is 1½ ins
Feeds on small insects and spiders
Young: usually twins

Big Brown Bat

The Big Brown Bat is one of the commonest bats in North America. It is both big and brown, although the shade of brown varies from region to region. It has a broad muzzle, and rounded ears and tragus. It flies very straight and fast. You are very likely to see this bat around buildings. Look for it near houses, barns, churches, and summer-houses. In summer, it gives birth in small groups or nurseries of up to 300 bats, and in winter it hibernates in buildings.

Bat
Length: 4–5 ins, of which tail is almost 2 ins
Feeds on insects, particularly large beetles
Young: 1–2 babies

Brazilian Free-tailed Bat

This is the most common and widespread free-tail bat—so called because its tail continues far beyond its tail membrane—but it is found only in the southern U.S., Mexico, and further south. Its short, thick fur is dark brown or grayish above. It sometimes roosts in buildings, but more often in caves. Thousands, or even millions, of these bats gather with their young in nursery roosts. You can tell if you are near one of their roosts by its musky smell. At dusk, so many leave the cave together to feed that they look like a plume of smoke from a distance. They fly high and fast, sometimes travelling several miles to feed. In winter, they migrate south up to 1,000 miles away.

Bat
Length: about
4 ins, of which
tail is 1½ ins
Feeds mostly on
small moths
Young: one baby

Mule Deer

You may see this deer almost anywhere in the prairies, desert scrub, forests, and mountains of western North America. Its fur is yellowish brown or reddish brown. Look for the black tip on its tail to tell it apart from the White-tailed Deer. Its ears are long like a mule's ears, and its rump (hind part) is white. Mule Deer are most active early in the morning, in the evening, and on moonlit nights. Like many other deer, each buck (male) tries to attract a herd of does (females) in the fall to mate. This is called the rutting season. You can tell the bulls by their antlers, although they lose them in January or February.

Ungulate
Length: 3½ ft, of which tail is 5–9 ins
Feeds on herbs and grasses in summer, shrubs, saplings, acorns, and fungi in winter
Tracks: 2–toed hooves
Young: 1–3 fawns

White-tailed Deer

You may see this deer anywhere in southern Canada and the U.S., except in the far West. It is similar to the Mule Deer, but its tail is white underneath and has no black on it, and its ears are smaller. When White-tailed Deer are alarmed, they snort and often stick their tails in the air. Only the bucks have antlers. They mate in the fall but, unlike most deer, some bucks mate only with one doe. The fawns are born in the spring, and are able to follow their mothers after only a few days. Their fur is heavily spotted. Fully-grown deer can run at 35–40 mph, and jump a gap of up to 30 ft.

Ungulate
Length:
4½–6½ ft,
of which tail is
6–13 ins
Feeds on grasses,
shrubs, trees, and
other plants
Tracks: 2–toed
hooves
Young: 1–3 fawns

Found in Many Habitats

Short-tailed Weasel

Carnivore: Weasel family
Length: 7½–13 ins, of which tail is 1½–3½ ins
Feeds mainly on mice and voles, but also eats birds, shrews, squirrels, and young rabbits
Tracks: 5 toes with central pad – Young: one litter of 6–9 babies

Short-tailed Weasels are found in most of Canada, Alaska, near the Great Lakes, and in New England. In summer, they are brown on top and white underneath. In winter, many northern animals become white all over except for the black tip on their tails. They are also called Ermines, and are sometimes hunted for their white winter fur. Short-tailed Weasels are most active at night, and hunt mainly on the ground. They do climb trees to prey on nesting birds. Listen out for their shrill shriek as they seize their prey. They dig a burrow under rocks, tree stumps or old buildings.

Badger

Badgers are found from the western U.S. to the Great Lakes, and in southwestern Canada. They are most active at night, but you may see one beside the highway early in the morning. You will easily recognize one from its stout, squat body, small head, and broad black stripes running down its white face. Badgers have long, strong claws which they use for digging out prey and their dens. You can tell a Badger's den by the pile of soil in front.

Carnivore: Weasel family
Length: 22–33 ins, of which tail is 4–6 ins
Feeds mainly on small mammals, such as ground squirrels, prairie dogs, gophers, mice, and rodents, but also on snakes and insects
Tracks: 5 toes with long claws and central pad
Young: one litter of 2–5 babies

Long-tailed Weasel

Long-tailed Weasels are found in southern Canada and over most of the U.S., except for the extreme Southwest. They look very like Short-tailed Weasels except that they are bigger, and their tails are longer. Males of both species are much larger than females. They are most active at night, and live in any kind of habitat, provided it is close to water. Although they spend most time on the ground, they do climb trees to prey on birds. They make nests under piles of wood or rocks, often in the old burrows of other animals. In winter their coats turn completely white.

Carnivore: Weasel family
Length: 11–22 ins, of which tail is 3–6 ins
Feeds on small mammals, including rabbits and squirrels, and birds, including poultry
Tracks: 5 toes with central pad
Young: one litter of 6–9 babies

Red Fox

Red Foxes are sleek, slender animals which look rather like small dogs. Their fur is reddish brown on top and white below, and their long, bushy tails have a white tip. Look for them in woods or forests throughout North America, except in the Southwest. Also, they can be seen in the suburbs of towns, on golf courses, and in cemeteries. They are most active at night, but you may see one in the early morning. Listen out at night for their drawn-out, high-pitched barking. During the day, Red Foxes may sleep out in the open, but they dig a den in sloping ground for their litters (young). Look out for fox droppings. They often contain fur, feathers, and broken bones—the parts of their prey they could not digest.

Carnivore: Dog family
Length: 2½–3½ ft, of which tail is 12–17 ins
Feeds on small mammals, birds, fruit, and insects
Tracks: 4 toes and pad
Young: usually one litter of 5–7 cubs

Gray Fox

Gray Foxes are found in southeastern Canada and throughout the U.S. except in the Plains and Rockies. They are similar in shape to a Red Fox, but their fur is grizzled grey on top with an orangy band around the sides. Their tails have a black stripe down the middle, but no white tip. The Gray Fox is a secretive animal, and is most active at night. It likes to live where there are plenty of trees or scrubby bushes, and will climb into a tree to escape from danger. It builds a den in a hollow tree, or thicket, or under a boulder.

Carnivore: Dog family
Length: 2½–3½ ft, of which tail is 8½–17 ins
Feeds on small mammals, birds, insects, and fruit
Tracks: 4 toes and pad
Young: usually one litter of 4 cubs

Coyote

Coyotes are larger than foxes and smaller than wolves, but they look similar to both. They are easily confused with dogs, especially "Coydogs," which are half-Coyote, half-dog. Coyotes are very adaptable, and can live in mountains, deserts, and even in the center of cities. You may see them anywhere in North America, except in the extreme north. They are most active at night. Listen for them howling and "yipping" at dusk and dawn. They are true scavengers (will eat almost anything they find).

Carnivore: Dog family
Length: 3¹/₂–4 ft, of which tail is 12–15 ins
Feeds on dead animals, mammals up to sheep
or deer, rabbits, poultry, frogs, and melons
Tracks: 4 toes with central pad
Young: one litter of 1–9 pups

Racoon

Racoons are one of the best-known carnivores in North America. You cannot miss their striped tails and the black mask of fur around their eyes. You may see them near the highway throughout southern Canada and the U.S., except for the highest parts of the Rockies. They are most active at night, but can be seen during the day. Racoons will eat almost anything. In cities, they live in storm drains, and raid garbage cans. In the country, they like to feed along streams and lakes. They make a den in a hollow tree or in a crack in the rocks, or may dig a burrow. When it gets very cold, they become sleepy, or sluggish.

Carnivore: Racoon family
Length: 2–3 ft, of which tail is 8–16 ins
Feeds on all kinds of food,
including fruit, crabs, frogs,
birds, insects, and rodents
Tracks: 5 toes
Young: usually one litter of
2–5 babies

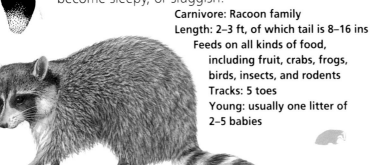

Brown Rat

A Brown Rat's fur is grayish brown, with a greasy sheen. Its tail is like the Black Rat's tail, only shorter. Brown Rats came originally from Siberia and China, and were brought to North America in ships. It is now only too common in cities, farms, and wherever there are people. In some cities there may be one Brown Rat for every five people. They live in sewers, and burrow under garbage dumps and along the foundations of buildings. They live in colonies, and are active mainly at night. Be careful: Brown Rats are pests that carry disease.

Rodent
Length: 12–18 ins, of which nearly half is the tail
Feeds on almost anything
Tracks: 4 toes on front feet, 5 on back feet
Young: up to 12 litters, each with 7–11 babies

Black Rat

Rodent
**Length: 12–17 ins, of which
tail is more than half**
Feeds on anything it can find
Tracks: 4 toes on front feet, 5 on back feet
Young: usually several litters a year, each with 7–8 babies

Black Rats have been accidentally introduced into North America from Europe and Asia. They still come here on ships. Although they are most common around ports, they have spread to some inland cities and farm buildings. They are usually only found where there are people, and damage food stores in such places as warehouses and barns. They climb well, both up trees and buildings. They have grayish brown fur, and a long, scaly tail. Be careful: Black Rats are pests that carry disease.

Bobcat

Bobcats are found over southern Canada and most of the U.S., except the Midwest. They are medium sized with cat-like faces, and thick, yellow-brown fur above, flecked with black. They have short tails, and can easily be confused with a Lynx (see page 26). They can adapt to many kinds of habitats, and are often found on the edges of towns where there is plenty of cover. They are most active at night and are seldom seen. Look for their tracks instead. They make a den in a hollow tree or a crack in the rocks.

Carnivore: Cat family
Length: 2–4 ft, of which tail is 3 1/2–8 ins
Feeds on small mammals and birds
Tracks: 4 toes with central pad
Young: usually a litter of 3–4 kittens

Mountain Lion

Mountain Lions can also be called Cougars, Pumas, Painters or Panthers, depending on where you are. They are easy to recognize with their buff-colored coats and lion's faces. They like wild country, such as mountains, marshes, and forests, and may be found in most of western North America, with a few in the Appalachians and in Florida. You are most likely to see one where there are plenty of deer. It makes its den in a cave or other sheltered place among the rocks, and marks its territory with scrapes (piles of twigs, grass, and other material).

Carnivore: Cat family
Length: 5–9 ft, of which tail is 20–36 ins
Feeds mostly on mammals, such as deer, beaver, porcupines, rabbits, and sometimes sheep
Tracks: 4 toes with central pad
Young: a litter of 2–4 cubs every second year

Southern Flying Squirrel

This tiny squirrel has thick, soft fur which is gray on top and white below. Down each side of its body it has a fold of loose skin that stretches between its front and back feet and allows it to glide from tree to tree. Although Southern Flying Squirrels are found all over the eastern U.S., they are not often seen because they are active only at night. They hoard food for the winter. They do not hibernate, but stay in their nests in old woodpecker holes, in bird boxes, or in house attics during bad weather.

Rodent: Squirrel family
Length: 8–9½ ins, of which nearly half is the tail
Feeds on seeds, nuts, insects, and birds' eggs
Young: usually 2 litters, each with 2–3 babies

Pygmy Shrew

The Pygmy Shrew is the smallest mammal in North America. It is found throughout most of Canada, parts of northern U.S., and in the Appalachians. You can tell it is a shrew by its long, pointed nose and small, beady eyes. Like all shrews, its ears are almost totally hidden in its fur. It is a very busy little animal, and is active both during the day and at night, but they are seldom seen. Look among leaf litter (leaves on the forest floor) and grass for their tiny tunnels, no more than an inch wide.

Insectivore
Length: 2½–4½ ins, of which tail is about 1 ins
Feeds on insects, their larvae, and worms
Tracks: 5 toes
Young: probably several litters, each with 3–8 babies

Eastern Mole

The Eastern Mole is found in the East of North America. This small black animal lives most of its life underground, so you will be lucky to see one. It has broad front feet for digging through the soil and, because it hardly ever needs to see, tiny eyes which are covered with thick skin. As it builds its tunnels it pushes out the loose soil from time to time, so making molehills. Some of the tunnels are as deep as 3 ft, but if you see a line of broken grass and soil, you will know there is a tunnel close to the surface. Moles are active during both day and night, and all through the winter. They love vegetable gardens.

Insectivore
Length: 3½–8 ins, of which tail is about 1 ins
Feeds mainly on earthworms – Young: one litter of 2–5 babies

Western Chipmunk

There are about sixteen different species of Western Chipmunk. They are usually smaller than the Eastern Chipmunk and not so gray. They all have different patterns of black and white stripes on their backs and faces, and are difficult to tell apart.

Rodent: Squirrel family
Length: 6½–12½ ins, of which tail is 2½–5½ ins
Feeds on seeds and other plant material, also insects
Tracks: 4 toes
Young: 1 or 2 litters, each with 2–7 babies

You can recognize a chipmunk by its bushy tail, big ears, and striped back. When it runs, it holds its tail straight up. Eastern Chipmunks are found in the East from southeastern Canada to northern Florida. They have a dark stripe down the middle of their backs, and a white stripe between two black stripes on each side. The best place to look for them is in open woodland. Listen out for their chip and chuck calls. Chipmunks fill their cheek pouches with food until they are bursting, then take the food back to their burrows. They dig their own burrows under the ground with a chamber for storing food. They sleep at night and are active during the day. In winter, they hibernate, waking occasionally to feed.

Eastern Chipmunk

Rodent: Squirrel family
Length: 8½–11½ ins, of which tail is 3–4 ins
Feeds on nuts, seeds and other parts of plants, snails, and insects
Tracks: 4 toes
Young: 2 litters of 2–8 babies

Striped Skunk

This is probably the best-known mammal in all of North America—it is black with broad white stripes down its back. Its white fur begins as a narrow stripe up its forehead, broadens into a white band on its neck, then divides into two broad stripes. Striped Skunks live in deserts, woods, farms, and even in your backyard. You will probably smell one before you see it. It hunts mainly at night, and digs a den in the ground, under abandoned buildings, boulders or piles of wood. It does not hibernate, but several females may share a den in winter.

Carnivore: Weasel family
Length: 20–30 ins, of which tail is 6½–15 ins
Feeds mostly on insects, eggs, and small mammals, as well as fruit and plants
Tracks: 5 toes with central pad
Young: one litter of 2–10 babies (usually 5–7)

Eastern Cottontail

The Eastern Cottontail is the most common rabbit in eastern North America. You will also see it in parts of Southwest U.S. It is easy to recognize from its long ears, long back legs, and short, cottony, white tail. Its fur is brownish above and white below. It feeds from early evening until late morning. Look for its droppings where it has been feeding. Most Cottontails do not burrow, but hide during the day in a slight dip in the ground close to thick grass or a fallen log for extra cover. When she gives birth, the female makes a nest of leaves and grasses lined with fur in a shallow dip.

Rabbit family
Length: 12–19 ins, of which tail is about 2 ins
Feeds on grasses in summer, twigs, and shoots in winter
Tracks: 4 toes surrounded by foot
Young: up to 7 litters, each with 1–7 babies

Gray Squirrel

Gray Squirrels are very well known in eastern North America from southern Canada to eastern Texas. Look for the long, bushy tail, gray upper fur, and white underparts. You will see them in woods, parks, and often in your own backyard. They build a nest in a tree hole or with leaves in the branches. Although they come down to the ground, they never stray far from a tree. They are active during the day, even in winter. In fall, you may notice a Gray Squirrel hiding acorns and nuts one at a time in the ground. Many of these buried nuts are never found—they grow into new trees.

Rodent: Squirrel family
Length: 17–19 ins, of which tail is about half
Feeds on nuts, berries, buds, bark, and eggs
Tracks: 4 toes on front feet, 5 toes on back feet
Young: 1 or 2 litters, each with 2–3 babies

Golden Mouse

Rodent – Length: 5½–7 ins, of which tail is nearly half
Feeds on seeds mostly, but also other plant material and insects
Tracks: 4 toes on front feet, 5 toes on back feet
Young: usually several litters, each with 2–3 babies

You can tell this from the Deer Mouse by its beautifully colored fur: bright golden cinnamon on top, with white below. The Golden Mouse is found in many habitats, but only in the southeastern U.S. It makes its home in boulder-strewn hillsides, trees, vines, and in brush, and wraps its tail around stalks and twigs to help it climb. It makes a nest of leaves and shredded bark, and may share it with other mice. It is most active at night.

Woodchuck

Woodchucks are also known as Groundhogs. They are found over most of Alaska, Canada, and the eastern U.S., in woods, meadows, and fields. A Woodchuck has a stocky body, short legs and ears, and a short, bushy tail. Its brownish fur is grizzled with gray. Listen for its whistle when it is alarmed, and for its growls and chatters when disturbed. Although they come above ground for only an hour or two each day, you are very likely to see one in the late afternoon, sunning itself near the entrance to its burrow. It usually digs its burrow near those of other Woodchucks, and each burrow may have as many as eleven entrances.

Rodent: Squirrel family
Length: 16–26 ins, of which tail is 4–6 ins
Feeds on grasses, clover, and other plants
Tracks: 4 toes on front feet, 5 toes on back feet
Young: one litter of 4–5 babies

Deer Mouse

You can tell this is a mouse by its large ears and eyes, and long tail. It can be seen over most of North America in all kinds of habitat from deserts to wet woodlands. Its fur varies in color from dark brown to yellowish above, and white below. Most active at night, it stores its uneaten food—it makes the largest stores in fall. It builds its nest in a hole in the ground or a tree, or in a bird's old nest.

Rodent
Length: 4½–11 ins, of which tail is 1½–6 ins
Feeds on nuts, berries, seeds, and insects
Tracks: 4 toes on front feet, 5 toes on back feet
Young: up to 4 litters or more, each with 1–9 babies

House Mouse

Rodent
Length: 5–7 ins, of which half is the tail
Feeds mostly on seeds, including grain
Tracks: 4 toes on front feet, 5 toes on back feet
Young: up to 13 litters, each with 3–12 babies

Some House Mice live outside in open scrub, but most prefer to live in and around houses and farm buildings. The House Mouse is probably the best-known rodent over most of North America. Its fur is dull gray-brown above, and only slightly paler below. A Deer Mouse has a white underside. It is most active at night. The first sign that there are mice in your house will probably be their small black droppings in a cupboard or place where there is food. They will eat almost anything, and can do an immense amount of damage in food stores.

Encouraging Bats

Bats roost during the day by hanging upside-down in a dark, quiet place. Many roost in trees, mine shafts, and caves. But as these are cut down or filled in, some now roost in buildings instead. Look for signs of them around your home and encourage them to come by putting up a few bat boxes (see right.)

Around the house

The picture shows how bats can get into your house and where they may be roosting. You will probably not even know they are there. They are so small that they can creep through cracks and holes no more than 3/4 inch wide.

If you see bats flying around your house at dusk, look for bat droppings in the attic or on a window sill. (They look like mouse droppings, but are crumbly.) If you think you have found a roost, do not disturb it. Call your local bat group (see page 78) who will send someone round to confirm that you are right and to identify the species of bat.

Bats and their roosts

You should not disturb bats or their roosts (the places where they rest and sleep.) During the year bats use several different roosts. In summer, mothers group together to give birth and to look after their babies. They like a warm roost for this and many bats may cram into one small box. In winter, bats may fly many miles away to hibernate in much cooler roosts.

Bats will roost in almost any part of a roof. They are quite likely not to come into the roof space at all, but if they do, put a sheet under their roost to catch the droppings.

Finding their way

Most animals that hunt at night have large eyes to see in the dark, but a bat uses its ears instead. As it flies it makes high-pitched squeaks. The bat listens for the echoes as these sounds bounce off objects around it. It can tell the shape of things and how close they are. The squeaks bats make are much too high for humans to hear, but you can buy a bat detector which will pick them up and help you identify them. Bat detectors are, however, expensive.

Make a bat box

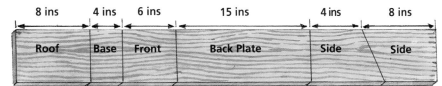

8 ins	4 ins	6 ins	15 ins	4 ins	8 ins
Roof	Base	Front	Back Plate	Side	Side

1 **Buy a piece of wood** that is at least 45 ins long, 6 ins wide and 1 ins thick. Make sure it has not been treated with wood preserver because that is poisonous to bats.

Where to hang the bat box

Your bat box should be at least 5 feet above the ground. Ask an adult to help you position it as high as you safely can on the south side of a tree or your house. The best time to put up your bat box is in spring.

The more bat boxes you can put up, the better chance you have of attracting bats, but you must be patient. It may take several months for a bat to find your box. If you have no luck after a year, move them somewhere else.

2 **Ask an adult to saw the wood into pieces,** as shown above.
3 **Scratch the wood for the back plate with a nail** so that it is rough enough for the bats to hang onto with their claws.
4 **Nail the sides to the front** so that the sides slope down to the front.
5 **Now nail the base to the sides and front.**
5 **Nail the sides to the back.** There should be a slit about 2 ins wide between the base and the back.
6 **Nail the roof to the wall tops.**
7 **Nail a piece of roofing felt over the joint** between the back plate and the roof to stop water getting in.

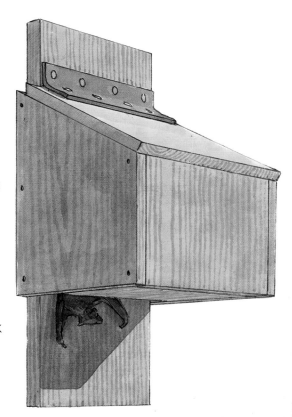

21

Woods & Forests

There are many different kinds of forest in North America. Coniferous forests cover much of the North, while western California and Oregon have tall redwood forests. There are cypress swamp forests in southern Georgia, and oak and pine forests in Florida.

Trees once covered most of North America east of the Appalachian Mountains, but by 1900 settlers had cleared most of the land as far north as New England. The forests which grow there now are new forests. Many native mammals depended on the original mix of trees. Some have disappeared altogether, while others, particularly bats, are now much rarer.

Old forests provide a much wider range of habitats. Mixed woods are good places for animals to live. They can make a nest or den among the shrubs, under the ground, or high in the trees. Bats roost in tree holes and hollow trees. Rodents feed on berries and nuts. Pine martens, lynx, and other carnivores prey on the rodents.

It is often difficult to spot woodland animals as many of them are active at night. Clearings, where a large tree has fallen, and woodland streams are good places to look for tracks, fur, partly eaten food, and droppings. Look in older trees too for holes which open into animal homes. The picture shows nine mammals from this book. How many can you recognize?

Red Bat, Elk, Snowshoe Hare, Lynx, Pine Marten, Virginia Opossum, Porcupine, Fox Squirrel, Gray Wolf.

Red Bat

Red Bats get their name from their brick-red fur which is much brighter in the males than the females. Both have white patches on their shoulders and white tips on their backs and bellies. They are found over most of eastern North America and in the extreme West and Southwest. They roost in tree holes and behind bark, or you may see one hanging among the leaves. Red Bats live on their own, and are difficult to see because they do not emerge from their roosts until it is nearly completely dark. They hunt over trees, flying fast, but steadily. The northernmost groups migrate south in the fall.

Bat
Length: 3½–4½ ins, of which tail is 1½–2½ ins
Feeds on insects
Young: usually 1–4 babies

Silver-haired Bat

You can see these bats in most of the U.S. and southern Canada. A Silver-haired Bat will come out fairly early in the evening, and hunt on its own. Look for it flying slowly, high above the trees. It gets its name from the silver tips which give its almost black fur a frosted look. It roosts under the bark of trees and in woodpecker holes. They sometimes collide with very tall buildings and radio towers. In winter, they migrate south, possibly in groups, to hibernate. They usually hibernate under bark, but some do hibernate in caves and mines.

Bat – Length: 3½–4 ins, of which tail is about 1½ ins
Feeds on moths, flies, and other flying insects
Young: twins

Moose

The Moose is the largest deer in the world. The top of its shoulders is over 6 ft high, and it can weigh over 1,200 lbs. Males are larger than females, and have huge, flat antlers up to 6 ft or more across, which they shed in winter. Look for the long flap of skin that hangs from their throats. Moose are found across most of Canada and south through the Rockies. They may be seen at any time of the day, although they are most active at night. Listen for the loud, bellowing call of the stage (male). In fall, adult moose gather in groups to mate. You may see lone stags or hinds (females) looking for mates.

Ungulate
Length: 6½–9 ft, of which tail is 6½ ins
Feeds on leaves of willows, aspen, birch, and other trees that grow near water
Tracks: 2-toed hooves
Young: 1–3 calves

Townsend's Big-eared Bat

Townsend's Big-eared Bat has enormous ears—up to 1¹/₂ ins long. When it is resting it folds them back over its neck or coils them like rams' horns, and unfurls them when it is disturbed. This bat is common in the West, but it is endangered in the East where there are scattered populations to Virginia. They emerge after dusk, and hover over the trees picking off moths. In June, the females form colonies of up to 1,000 bats to give birth to their young, and remain together to look after

Bat
Length: 3¹/₂–4 ins, of which tail is 1¹/₂–2 ins
Feeds on moths and other insects
Young: one baby

them. In winter, they again form large colonies to hibernate in caves, tightly packed together. (For more about bats, see pages 10 and 20–21.)

Mountain Beaver

A Mountain Beaver does not always live in mountains, and is not closely related to beavers. It is about as large as a rabbit, and is brownish black with small eyes and short, rounded ears. It has short legs and almost no tail. It lives in wet forests close to streams in the extreme West of the U.S. from British Columbia to northern California. Mountain Beavers are most active at night, and build long burrows into the banks of streams. The entrance to their burrows can be up to 18 ins across. In very wet places, they cover the entrance with twigs, leaves, and ferns up to 2 ft high.

Rodent – Length 9–18 ins, of which tail is 2 ins or less
Feeds on bark, twigs, berries, and pine needles
Tracks: 5 toes, webbed back feet
Young: one litter of 2–6 babies

Virginia Opossum

Opossums are the only marsupials (animals that carry their young in a pouch) in North America. The new-born young are tiny—the whole litter could fit in a teaspoon. They crawl into their mother's pouch and develop there for about two months. When the young possums leave their mother's pouch, they often travel on her back, gripping her tail with their own tail. Opossums are found in woods near fields in the eastern U.S., and have been introduced on the West Coast. You are most likely to see them on highways. An opossum has a pointed, white face and grizzled, grayish fur. Its tail has few hairs.

Marsupial
Length: 2–3 ft, of which tail is 9–21 ins
Feeds on fruit, vegetables, nuts, meat, eggs, insects, and carrion
Tracks: 5 toes spread wide
Young: usually 2 litters, each up to 21 babies

Gray Wolf

Gray Wolves used to roam over most of North America, but are now found only in Alaska, Canada, and the U.S. around the Great Lakes and in the Rockies. You will probably have to go to a very remote place to hear their long, deep howl. A Gray Wolf looks similar to a Coyote (see page 14), but it is larger and its bark is less yappy. The color of its fur may be anything from white to yellow to reddish brown to almost black. Wolves live in packs of about eight and hunt mainly at night. They often follow each other in a line, especially in the snow, stepping exactly on the tracks of their leader. The strongest male leads the pack.

Carnivore: Dog family
Length: 4–5³/₄ ft, of which tail is 13–19 ins
Feeds mostly on other mammals, even Moose and Caribou
Tracks: 4 toes with central pad
Young: one litter, usually of 6–7 cubs

Lynx

Lynxes look very like Bobcats (see page 15), and are easily confused with them. Lynxes, however, are found further north, from Alaska to Newfoundland. It is mainly around the U.S. border and the U.S. Rockies that the two species overlap. You will have to look carefully to see that a Lynx has bigger ear tufts and a black tip to its short tail. Lynxes like deep conifer forests where they hunt on their own and mainly at night. They have very large feet and so leave big tracks in the snow. They build a den in a hollow log, under roots, or other sheltered places.

Carnivore: Cat family
Length: 2–3¹/₂ ft, of which tail is only 2–5¹/₂ ins
Feeds on mammals, particularly snowshoe hares, and birds
Tracks: 4 toes with central pad
Young: one litter of 1–5 babies

Pine Marten

You can tell this is a weasel from its long, lithe body, short legs, and long, bushy tail. Its fur is a dark glossy brown or yellowish brown, with a buff or orange patch on its throat and chest. It lives mainly in conifer forests, throughout most of Canada and south into the U.S. Rockies and New England. Pine Martens are most active at night and spend much of their time hunting in trees, but they come down to the ground to forage for food, too. Their tracks are clearest in early spring and summer. In winter, their feet are covered in thick hair, and this tends to blur their footprints. They make a den in a hollow tree or log.

Carnivore: Weasel family
Length: 20–25 ins,
of which tail is 5½–9 ins
Feeds on small
mammals, birds,
insects, and fruit
Tracks: 5 toes
Young: one litter
of 1–5 babies

Fisher

Fishers look very like Pine Martens, but are larger, with dark brown to black fur. Notice too that Fishers have no throat or chest patch. They are found in much the same areas as Pine Martens, but are less widespread. Look for Fisher tracks in old, deep woods. Fishers are active both during the day and at night. They are equally at home in the trees and on the ground. They may make their den in a tree hollow, or in the cleft of a rock. If you see droppings with small porcupine quills in them, they will have been made either by a Fisher or a Coyote.

Carnivore: Weasel family
Length: 2½–3 ft, of which
tail is 12–16 ins
Feeds on mice and other small rodents,
porcupines, carrion, birds, fruit, and nuts
Tracks: 5 toes
Young: one litter of 1–5 babies

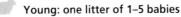

Woods & Forests

Red Squirrel

You will probably hear a Red Squirrel chattering and trilling before you see it. You can recognize it from its small size and its coat, which is reddish brown above and white below. Look for the tufts of hair on its ears and the black edging to its tail. You are most likely to see one in conifer forests in Alaska, Canada, the Rockies, or in the Appalachians. Look for discarded food piles of gnawed pine cones and acorns. It builds a drey (nest) of twigs in a treehole or on the ground. It does not hibernate in winter.

Rodent
Length: 11–15 ins, of which tail is 4–6 ins
Feeds mainly on pine nuts and other seeds, fungi, nuts, berries, small animals, and birds' eggs
Tracks: 4 toes on front, 5 toes on back feet
Young: usually 2 litters, each with 3–7 babies

Golden-mantled Ground Squirrel

It looks rather like a Western Chipmunk (see page 17), but it is found only in forests and on the stony slopes of the Rockies. It has no stripes across its face, but look for the two broad, white stripes on its sides. You are quite likely to see them around camp sites. Do not try to feed these squirrels as they can be rabid and they are disease carriers. They dig a deep burrow with its entrance near a bush, rock or log. They store food in their burrows, and hibernate during the winter.

Rodent – Length: 9–12 ins, of which tail is 2½–4½ ins
Feeds on seeds, nuts, leaves, fungi, and insects
Tracks: 4 toes on front, 5 toes on back feet
Young: one litter of 2–8 babies

Shrew Mole

Shrew Moles are the smallest moles in North America. They are found only on the West Coast from southern Canada to central California. A Shrew Mole looks rather like a shrew with its long, pointed nose, and its feet are not as big as those of other moles. Although it burrows, it often comes above ground, too. You may see it walking slowly and carefully through the leaf litter (leaves on the ground) in a forest. It feeds on insects it finds there.

Insectivore
Length: about 4½ ins, of which tail is 1½ ins
Feeds on insects, and also salamanders
Young: more than 1 litter a year, each with 1–4 babies

Southern Red-backed Vole

This little animal is common across most of Canada, and extends south into the Rockies, South Dakota, New England, and North Carolina. It is smaller than a lemming and has a longer tail. You can tell it from most other voles by its reddish brown back and gray sides. It likes forests with thick ground cover, particularly damp woods and bogs. It makes a nest under roots or logs, and stores food in the fall to see it through the winter.

Rodent
Length: 5–6 ins, of which tail is 1½ ins
Feeds on green plants, shoots, seeds, berries, and fungi
Tracks: 4 toes on front, 5 toes on back feet
Young: several litters a year, each with 3-4 babies

Fox Squirrels are the largest North American squirrels. Their large size is the best way to identify them. They are found all over eastern U.S. except in New England. The color of their coat is usually rusty brown above and orange below, but in Florida it is all black, in South Carolina it is black with white ears and nose, and in Maryland it is silvery gray with a white belly. Fox Squirrels have been introduced into parts of Canada and western U.S. They build their nest in a tree hole or in a hole in the ground.

Fox Squirrel

Rodent Squirrel family
Length: 17–27 ins, of which
tail is about half
Feeds on nuts, shoots,
buds, small animals,
and birds' eggs
Tracks: 4 toes on front,
5 toes on back feet
Young: 2 litters, each with 2–5 babies

Snowshoe Hare

Snowshoes are found throughout most of Alaska, Canada, and in the U.S. in the Rockies, New England, and Allegheny Mountains. In summer, their fur is rusty brown with white below, their short tails are white above, and their long ears are tipped with black. In winter, they are white all over except their ears still have black tips. Like all rabbits and hares, their feet are covered with hair. Snowshoes do not build nests, but lay up in shallow dips, called forms. Their young can open their eyes soon after birth, and are covered with fur.

Hare and Rabbit family
Length: 14–20 ins, of which tail is only 1–2 ins
Feeds on woody shrubs, clovers, grasses,
and other green plants
Tracks: 4 toes
Young: up to 4 litters,
each with 1–9 babies

Porcupine

The only mammal in North America to have quills, porcupines can be found in most of Canada, western U.S., and as far south as Pennsylvania in the East. They are most active at night, but you may see one lumbering through the forest or high in a tree, hunched into a large, black ball. They make a den in a hollow tree or in a cave in the rocks. Listen out for their grunts, groans, and high-pitched cries. Look for them along highways. A baby Porcupine's quills are soft when it is born, but harden within 15 minutes. Don't go near porcupines and keep your pets away from them, as they can have rabies.

Rodent – Length: 2–3 ft, of which tail is 6–11½ ins
Feeds on leaves, twigs, the bark of trees,
and some green plants
Tracks: 5 toes with a central pad – Young: one baby

Signs of Mammals

Most mammals keep well out of sight of people. If you want to see them, you should wear the right clothes and keep very quiet. Many mammals come out to feed at dusk and dawn—those are the best times to look for them. However, mammals leave lots of tracks and signs behind them which you can see at any time. Don't try to pet wild animals—some carry diseases dangerous to humans, and it is safer for them not to trust people.

What to look for

Animals move stealthily and swiftly, but they may leave behind any of the signs shown here. Many mammals burrow deep beneath the ground or into a bank. Look for the entrance hole and for tunnels and paths in the grass.

footprints   **half-eaten food**

Make an accident survey

Not much is known about how many mammals there are in a particular area. You can help by recording your sightings. Many of the mammals you see will be dead, killed by traffic on the roads. If you spot a dead animal, make a note of where it is (see Map Reading opposite) and record the details in your ring binder.

These dead animals are a useful way of finding out where mammals are living and help to estimate how many there are. You can also find out:
- Which mammal do you see dead most often?
- Does this vary depending on the time of year?

Map reading

The best way to pinpoint where you saw something is by giving its map reference. Maps are divided into squares by lines. Each line is numbered at the edges of the map. Suppose you spot a dead fox at the spot marked with an X. You can describe this place as "on Route 66, 3 miles east of Newtown," but it

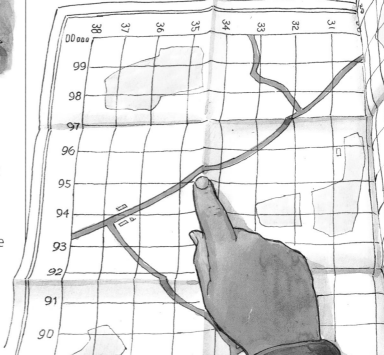

chewed bark

droppings

is much simpler to say "Ref: 4/H." To give a map reference:

1 **Find the place on the map.** Ask an adult to help you if you have problems with this.

2 **Look for the first vertical (up and down) line on its left.** Follow it up or down to the edge of the map and write it down in your notebook.

3 **Go back to the place on the map and find the first horizontal (across) line below it.**

4 **Follow this line to the nearest edge of the map** and write down its number after the first one with a slash (/) separating the number from the letter.

5 **When you make your permanent record,** list all the foxes on one page, give the date when you saw each one, and the map reference. Next do the gophers, and so on.

Clothes and equipment

Your best chance of spotting mammals is when they do not know you are there. As soon as they see or hear you, they are likely to run and hide. Wear dull-colored clothes and comfortable shoes, or rubber boots. Look for mammals in quiet, secret places such as ditches, hedges, and among thick undergrowth. The best way is to sit very quietly and listen. You do not need much equipment:

1 **A lightweight backpack** to hold all your equipment.

2 **A plastic garbage bag** is useful for sitting on if the ground is wet.

3 **Pencils, pens, and a field notebook** for drawing tracks and noting what you have seen.

4 **Tape measure or ruler** to measure the size of prints and the distance between them.

5 **Pair of binoculars** may be helpful if you are looking for deer.

6 **Plastic bags** are useful for collecting specimens.

7 **If you are planning to make plaster casts of tracks,** check you have everything you need (see page 49.)

8 **A camera** is useful to record interesting tracks, marks on trees, dens, and so on.

9 **Take a flashlight** if you are watching at dusk.

You can write up your records on a separate sheet of paper for each species when you get home. Glue your sketches, drawings of tracks from your field notebook, and photographs onto the sheet as well. Keep your records in a ring binder.

Grasslands & Savanna

**Wide, open grasslands once stretched
from the Appalachians to the Rockies,
covering much of North America. Most of
this land is now planted with crops, and
only bits of the original prairies remain.**

However, you will also find prairies in California,
the Southwest, and between the Rockies and the
Sierra Nevada. There are two kinds of grassland in
the Prairies: short grass in the West, changing to tall
grass in the East. Tall grass is spectacular in spring
when the wild flowers are out. It used to provide
grazing for huge herds of bison, pronghorn
(antelope,) and bighorn sheep. Short grass prairies
still stretch for many miles. They get less rain than
tall grass, but many small mammals such as jack-
rabbits, ground squirrels, and prairie dogs live there.
The picture shows seven mammals from this book.
How many can you recognize?

Bison (herd in distance,) Swift Fox, Prairie Dogs,
Pronghorns, White-tailed Jack Rabbit,
Spotted Skunk, Least Weasel.

Swift Fox

Swift Foxes are smaller than Gray and Red Foxes (see page 13) and, unlike them, their fur is a grayish-yellow color all over. Look for their big ears and the black tip at the end of their tails. Swift Foxes are found only in shortgrass prairies and in dry, desert plains. At one time, many were killed by poisonous baits left for Coyotes, but the numbers of Swift Foxes have begun to increase again in the last forty years. They hunt mainly at night, and spend most of the day in their burrows.

Carnivore: Dog family
Length: 2–2½ ft, of which tail is about a third
Feeds on small rodents, rabbits, birds, insects, berries, and grasses
Tracks: 4 toes – Young: one litter of 3–6 cubs

Black-footed Ferret

Black-footed Ferrets look similar to the ferrets sold in pet stores. Its face is a bit like a Racoon's with its black eye-mask, but its fur is mainly buff-colored. Look for its black feet and the black tip to its tail. It scarcely survives in the wild, and has been declared extinct several times, as the prairie dogs (see page 37) on which it preys have been destroyed by poisons. It makes its den under the ground. Black-footed Ferrets have been bred in captivity and released back into the wild, where it is hoped they will adapt.

Carnivore: Weasel family
Length: 18–22 ins, of which tail is a quarter
Tracks: 5 toes with central pad
Feeds on prairie dogs and other animals
Young: one litter of 3–5 babies

Least Weasel

The Least Weasel is the smallest carnivore in the world. Like other weasels, it has a long, lithe body and short legs, which allow it to chase mice and voles deep into their burrows. It kills its prey by biting through the base of its skull. A Least Weasel is brown above and white below with a short tail. It is found throughout Canada and parts of northern U.S., but is not common anywhere. It likes grassy fields and open woods close to rivers and marshes. It is most active at night when you may hear its shrill shriek.

Carnivore: Weasel family
Length: 7–8 ins, of which tail is about 1 ins
Tracks: 5 toes with central pad
Feeds mostly on small mice, voles, small rabbits, birds, and other animals
Young: 2 or 3 litters, each with 3–6 young

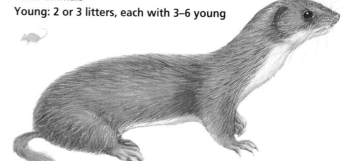

Bison

Bison are wild cattle with very powerful heads, shoulders, and front legs. Look for the big hump of their shoulders and the long, shaggy hair on their shoulders and front legs. Huge herds of Bison once roamed the plains of North America, but within fifty years they were almost all killed by hunters. Today, they are a protected species, and you can again see herds of Bison in parks and preserves, mainly in western North America. They like to scratch themselves by rubbing their horns and heads on a boulder or tree. Look for a ring of rubbed bark about 5 ft above the ground. They also like to roll in the dust—look for bare dips in the ground where they have wallowed.

Ungulate
Length: 6½–12 ft,
of which tail is 17–23 ins
Feeds mostly on grasses,
but also browses on shrubs
Tracks: 2-toed,
rounded hooves
Young: usually one calf

Mustang

Mustangs or Wild Horses look very similar to domestic ponies and horses, but their feet, of course, are unshod. Look for the V-shaped mark on their hoof print to tell them apart. Mustangs were protected in 1971, and they have become more common on the prairies since then. If you are lucky enough to be able to hide at a water hole at dawn, you may see Mustangs and Pronghorns coming to drink. Family groups usually consist of one stallion (male) and five or six mares (females). Stallions mark their territories by building up piles of droppings in selected places. Burros (asses which have returned to the wild) have shorter manes and tails than horses. They are more common in the Southwest of the U.S.

Ungulate – Length: 6½–7 ft, of which tail is 19 ins
Feeds on grasses and shrubby plants
Tracks: a circular hoof with V-shape – Young: usually one foal

Antelope

Antelopes, also known as Pronghorns, are the fastest animals on land in North America—they can run up to 40 m.p.h. Antelopes are not closely related to deer. They are sandy brown with a white belly and chest. The large patch of white on their rump (hind part) is the best way to tell them apart from Whitetail and Mule Deer. When a Pronghorn is alarmed, the white hairs on its rump stand up, making the patch look larger still. Both male and females have short, stout horns, although the females' are smaller than the males'. You will usually see Pronghorns in small bands on the prairies. The males each gather about twenty females around them. When the fawns are born, they are hidden separately by the mother until they join the herd a week later.

Ungulate
Length: 4–4½ ft, of which tail is 2½–6½ ins
Feeds on grasses, shrubs, and sometimes crops, such as alfalfa and wheat
Tracks: 2-toed hooves
Young: 1–3 fawns

Grasslands & Savanna

Spotted Skunk

The Spotted Skunk is a small, black skunk with white stripes or spots along its head, back and sides. Its tail has a white tip. When it is alarmed, it stands on its front feet and sprays a foul-smelling scent up to a distance of 13 ft. It will also climb trees to escape from danger, but spends most of the time on or under the ground. It is found across most of the U.S., except in New England and down the East Coast. It likes open places including farmland, scrub, and woods. It hunts at night, and digs a burrow under buildings or piles of rocks, and several skunks may share a den in winter.

Carnivore: Skunk family
Length: 13–22 ins, of which tail is 2½–8½ ins
Feeds on almost anything, particularly small mammals, insects, fruit, reptiles, and carrion
Tracks: 5 toes with central pad
Young: one litter of 4–5 babies

Hispid Cotton Rat

Hispid Cotton Rats have coarse blackish or dark grizzled-brown fur, with whitish bellies. Their ears are almost hidden by their fur, and their tails are fairly short and scaly. They are found in grassy fields in the southeastern U.S. Look for the runways they make through the grass, leaving small piles of cut grass stems along them. They make a nest on the surface or in a burrow. The young leave the nest before they are a week old, and can breed themselves when they are only six weeks old. Cotton Rats seldom live for more than a year, but they can cause a lot of damage to sugarcane, sweet potatoes and other crops.

Rodent
Length: 8–14 ins, of which tail is 3–6½ ins
Feeds on almost anything, including insects, crabs, birds and their eggs, and crops
Tracks: 4 toes on front, 5 toes on back feet
Young: several litters, each of 1–12 babies

Meadow Jumping Mouse

Rodent
Length: 7–10 ins, of which tail is more than half
Feeds on seeds, grasses, fungi, beetles, and other insects
Tracks: 4 toes on front, 5 toes on back feet
Young: 2 or 3 litters, each with 2–8 babies

This small mouse is darker above than below, and has long back legs and feet. When it is startled, it makes a few bounding jumps and then freezes. If you see it do this, you could possibly mistake it for a frog. They are found in meadows, marshes, and the edge of forests across most of Canada, and south into the U.S. to Oklahoma and Georgia. It is most active at night, and builds a nest below the ground in which it hibernates for up to eight months in winter. In April or May, it emerges and builds a nest on the surface of the ground or beneath a log or tree stump.

Black-tailed Prairie Dog

These prairie dogs are bigger than most other ground squirrels, but are slightly smaller than a cat. Their fur is pale yellowish brown above and whitish below. If you can get close enough to one, look at its tail to see if it has a black or white tip. Only the Black-tailed Prairie Dog has a black tip to its tail. Look for bare mounds of earth 10–20 yards apart and about 1–2 ft high. They are the sign that there is a prairie dog town under the ground. One animal keeps watch on a mound of earth while the rest of the group feeds. If the look-out spots danger it barks, and all the prairie dogs disappear underground. Many prairie dogs have been poisoned in places set aside for sheep and cows, and so there are many fewer of them than there used to be.

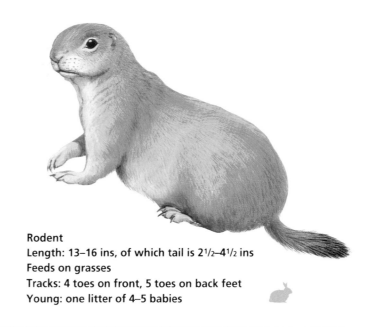

Rodent
Length: 13–16 ins, of which tail is 2½–4½ ins
Feeds on grasses
Tracks: 4 toes on front, 5 toes on back feet
Young: one litter of 4–5 babies

Thirteen-lined Ground Squirrel

This ground squirrel gets its name from the thirteen dark-brown and creamy–buff stripes down its back. Notice how the lighter stripes are often broken into spots. Unlike chipmunks (page 17), it has no stripes on its face. It lives on its own, and likes shortgrass prairies. If you live in central states, you may also come across one on a golf course, beside the road or even in your own backyard. Listen for its sharp alarm call, followed by a musical chattering when it is safely back in its shallow burrow. It hibernates between October and March.

Rodent
Length: 6½–11½ ins, of which tail is 2½–5 ins
Feeds on almost anything, particularly insects, grass, and other plants
Tracks: 4 toes on front, 5 toes on back feet
Young: one litter of 3–13 babies

Richardson's Ground Squirrel

Richardson's Ground Squirrel is one of the most common mammals on the shortgrass prairies and sagebrush scrub. Its fur is smoky gray mixed with buff. Its long tail is edged with white or buff. Like most other ground squirrels, they dig burrows in the ground and live close to each other in loose colonies. Watch for one standing on its back legs, looking out for intruders. And listen for its warning whistle which sends all the others fleeing back to their burrows. Richardson's Ground Squirrels store food in their burrows. The adults sleep through the hottest summer months (estivate) until September, and hibernate through the coldest winter months. Like other ground squirrels they are known to carry plague.

Rodent
Length: 10–14 ins, of which tail is 2½–3½ ins
Feeds mostly on grass, roots, and other plants, including crops
Tracks: 4 toes on front, 5 toes on back feet
Young: usually one litter of 2–11 babies

White-tailed Jack Rabbit

Rabbit and Hare family
Length: 22–25 ins, of which tail is 2½–4 ins
Feeds on grasses, clovers, crops, twigs, and bark shoots
Tracks: 4 toes on front, 5 toes on back feet;
back prints are much longer than front ones
Young: 1 or 2 litters, each with 3–6 babies

Like other rabbits and hares, the White-tailed Jack Rabbit has long ears and a short tail. Its fur is grayish brown in summer, but pale gray in winter. The best way to tell it from other jack rabbits is to look at its tail, which is white both above and below. White-tailed Jack Rabbits are found in open plains and pastures mainly in the U.S. from California to Iowa. They have long legs, and you may see them fleeing at high speed through the grass. If they are chased, they will run in a huge circle, a mile or more across. They can also jump a gap of up to 17 ft. They forage for food at night and, unless disturbed, sit in their lairs during the day. They do not burrow into the ground, but they make tunnels in deep snow.

Western Pocket Gopher

This gopher has a large, blunt head and short legs. It has fur-lined pouches in each cheek which it packs with food to take back to the nest. The claws on the front feet are long and curved, and very useful for digging burrows. You can tell if there are gophers about because they push fan-shaped mounds of earth up to the surface as they burrow. Western Pocket Gophers live on their own for most of their lives, and are active during the day and at night. They are seldom seen above ground, but will sometimes come to the surface to forage for plants, which they bite off below ground level and then drag into their tunnels. Although they may damage crops, they probably do more good to the soil than harm. Slightly different species of Western Pocket Gopher live in different regions in the western U.S.

Rodent – Length: 5–10½ ins, of which tail is 2–3½ ins
Feeds on plants, bulbs, and roots
Tracks: 4 toes on front,
5 toes on back feet
Young: 1 or 2 litters,
each with 1–10
babies

Eastern Pocket Gophers

The only difference between Eastern Pocket Gophers and Western Pocket Gophers is that the former have grooves down the center of their teeth, but you are hardly likely to see those. Like the Western animals, the color of their fur varies from one region to another. Notice their small eyes and ears, surrounded by short, thick fur, and the long claws on their front feet. They like loose, sandy soils best in which to dig their burrows. In winter, they tunnel through the snow, and push loose dirt from the ground underneath into these tunnels. When the snow melts, look for the long "ropes" of dirt that remain on the surface of the ground.

Rodent
Length: 7–14 ins, of which tail is 2–4½ ins
Feeds on plants, particularly roots and bulbs
Tracks: 4 toes on front, 5 toes on back feet
Young: several litters, each with 1–8 babies

Southeastern Pocket Gopher

Plains Pocket Gopher

Southern Bog Lemming

This small lemming looks very like a Field Vole, but its tail is even shorter and its fur is more brownish than grayish. It is found in much of eastern North America from Quebec to North Carolina. In spite of its name, it likes grassy meadows, not bogs or marshes. It is active during the day and at night. Like Field Voles, it makes runways through the grass, and leaves piles of cut grass stems along them where it has been feeding. Look for its bright green droppings. It may build its nest of grass above the ground or in a burrow.

Rodent
Length: 4½–6 ins, of which tail is ½–1 ins
Feeds on leaves, grass seed, moss, fungi, and some insects
Tracks: 4 toes on front, 5 toes on back feet spread wide
Young: several litters, each with 3–5 babies

Nine-banded Armadillo

It is easy to recognize a Nine-banded Armadillo: it is the only mammal in North America to have a hard, "armored" shell. It can curl up inside it when it is threatened, but it usually dashes for safety into its burrow or thick bushes. Notice that the top of its head and its tail are protected as well as its body. Armadillos belong to South America, and originally were found only in the extreme Southeast of the U.S. They have spread farther, however, and are now found in crop fields as far north as Georgia.

You are most likely to see an armadillo early in the morning or in the evening. Watch it snuffling in the leaf mold for food. You may also see it rolling in mud at a water hole or by a stream.

Insectivore
Length: 2–2½ ft, of which tail is 9½–14 ins
Feeds on insects and other small animals, such as frogs, reptiles, birds, and eggs
Tracks: 4 toes on front feet, 5 toes on back feet
Young: one litter of 4 babies from one cell

Harvest Mouse

Harvest Mice look very like House Mice (see page 19). Their fur is usually brownish above and white below, and they have big ears and eyes, and a long tail. Unlike House Mice, Harvest Mice have a groove down their upper teeth. Harvest Mice climb well, but are hard to spot among the vegetation. Look instead for their round nest of grasses. They may build them on the ground, or above ground, in vines, bushes, and woodpecker holes. They breed throughout the year except in the north, where they breed in the warm months.

Rodent
Length: 4–7½ ins, of which tail is nearly half
Feeds mostly on seeds and plants
Tracks: 4 toes on front, 5 toes on back feet
Young: several litters, each with 1–9 babies

Short-tailed Shrew

You can tell this is a shrew by its long, pointed nose, small eyes, and soft, velvety fur. As its name implies, its tail is shorter than most other shrews. Its saliva (spit) is poisonous, and one bite is usually enough to paralyze its prey. They are found in woods, swamps, and bogs, as well as in grasslands, over the eastern U.S. and north into eastern Canada. They are very busy animals, and are active during the day as well as at night, hunting for food and tunnelling in the ground or under the snow. They also use tunnels and runways made by mice and other small rodents.

Insectivore
Length: 3½–5½ ins, of which tail is about 1 ins
Feeds on insects, worms, snails, and young mice
Tracks: 4 toes
Young: up to 3 litters, each with 3–7 babies

Field Vole

You can tell voles or lemmings from mice and rats because voles and lemmings have small ears and eyes, and shorter tails. Field Voles have grayish fur and are found in grassy areas all over Canada and in most of the U.S. Look in long grass for signs of them—they make little paths radiating out through the grass from their burrows. Look for piles of cut grass stems along their runways. In winter, look for Field Voles' tooth marks on the bark of bushes. Like gophers (see page 39) they tunnel through the snow in winter, filling the tunnels with grass, dirt, and sticks, which are revealed when the snow melts. In summer, they dig burrows under the ground, although some build their round nests in plants overhanging a stream and swim to and from the nest. Weasels prey on voles, and may take over their nest and line it with their victims' fur.

Rodent – Length: 4–10 ins, of which tail is 1–4½ ins
Feeds on plants, particularly grass, twigs, roots, and bulbs
Tracks: 4 toes on front feet, 5 toes on back feet spread wide
Young: several litters, each with up to 12 babies

Hunting for Hunters

Many carnivores (meat-eaters) hunt at night and live alone. These animals are often difficult to see. Look out for their dens and burrows instead, as well their tracks and droppings, bits of fur, and other signs they leave behind them.

Otters

Look for signs of otters along lake sides and river banks in wooded country. Otters are playful creatures—sometimes they make a slide down a muddy bank straight into the water. They regularly leave their droppings in very obvious places, on logs and large stones, often near the entrance to their holt (den).

Otter droppings are called "spraints." They are tarry black when fresh, with a strong, sweet smell. As they dry, they turn white and look like piles of cigar ash. If you break one open with a twig, you may see fish scales and bones in them. (Wash your hands after you have done this.) If you find a dropping that smells nasty, it will have come from a mink.

Badger's sett

If you see a mound of earth in front of the entrance to a large den, it probably belongs to a badger. Look around the entrance for other signs. Badgers are very clean animals. They use a special place or hollow as a latrine for their droppings.

Look for dry grass, leaves, and other bedding which the badger has dropped as it takes them to its den. Examine nearby trees for scratch marks where the badger has cleaned its claws. It also rubs its fur on the bark. Can you find any hairs or dirt sticking to the bark?

Caught on the wire

As animals crawl through barbed wire, some of their hair may get caught in it. You will easily find sheep's wool in spiky bushes and barbed wire, but look for the fur of rabbits and badgers as well.

Whose hole in the ground?

Foxes, badgers, and other carnivores dig dens into the ground or under thick bushes. The size of the hole is a good clue to its maker. Fox and badger holes are about 1 foot high. Rabbit holes are about 4 inches high. Vole and mouse holes are about 2 inches.

Tracks

Foxes and cats all leave paw prints with four toes, rather like those of a dog. Notice how the toes are arranged around the central pad to tell them apart. Members of the weasel family, including badgers, leave five-toed prints. If the tracks are clear, you can often tell more from them than simply which animal has made them.

- Can you tell those made by the front feet from those of the back feet?
- How far apart are they?
- Do you think the animal was walking or running?
- Is there more than one set of prints? If so, was one animal chasing the other?
- Look to see if there is the mark of a long tail dragging on the ground.

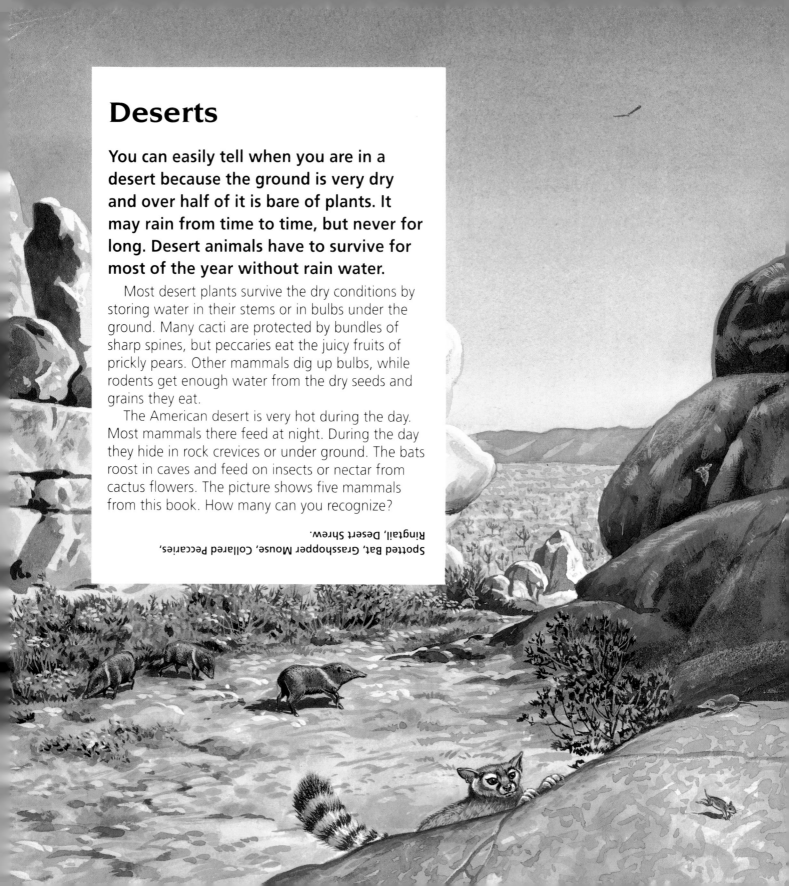

Deserts

You can easily tell when you are in a desert because the ground is very dry and over half of it is bare of plants. It may rain from time to time, but never for long. Desert animals have to survive for most of the year without rain water.

Most desert plants survive the dry conditions by storing water in their stems or in bulbs under the ground. Many cacti are protected by bundles of sharp spines, but peccaries eat the juicy fruits of prickly pears. Other mammals dig up bulbs, while rodents get enough water from the dry seeds and grains they eat.

The American desert is very hot during the day. Most mammals there feed at night. During the day they hide in rock crevices or under ground. The bats roost in caves and feed on insects or nectar from cactus flowers. The picture shows five mammals from this book. How many can you recognize?

Spotted Bat, Grasshopper Mouse, Collared Peccaries, Ringtail, Desert Shrew.

Sanborn's Long-nosed Bat

Sanborn's Long-nosed Bat is found only in the extreme south of Arizona and New Mexico, and only in the summer. It is a large bat with a long nose and no tail. If you see one close-to, look for the leaf-like flap of skin at the end of its nose. It comes to the U.S. from Mexico to mate and give birth—colonies of several thousand mothers gather with their babies in caves, mines, and tunnels. While the mothers go out to collect pollen from agave, saguaro, and organ pipe cactuses, the babies are left hanging on their own.

Bat
Length: about 3 ins
Feeds on nectar and pollen of cactuses
Young: 1–2 babies

Ghost-faced Bat

If you get the chance to look closely at this bat, you will see that it has leaf-like folds of skin across its chin. They stretch to its ears, and are not found on any other North American bat. Its fur is brownish. It is a strong flier, and you may see it in the deserts of Arizona, Texas, and Mexico. It likes to roost in caves and old mines, and particularly likes hot, humid sites. Although only a few roosting sites are known in Texas, some of them have several thousand bats in them. Further south, in Mexico, roosts have been found with up to half a million bats.

Bat
Length: up to 3¹/₂ ins
Feeds on insects, particularly moths
Young: one baby

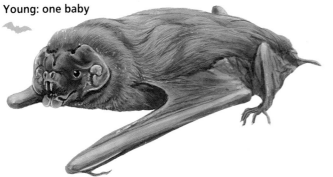

Spotted Bat

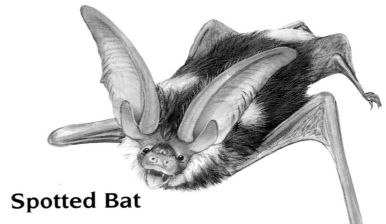

Spotted Bats are quite spectacular. They have huge, pink ears and three large, white spots on their dark brown backs. They have occasionally been found as far north as British Columbia and Montana, as well as in the desert further south. You will be very lucky to see one—it is one of the rarest bats in the U.S., and only fifteen were found in the seventy years before the 1960s. It likes rocky cliffs and dry areas near streams.

Bat
Length: 4¹/₂ ins, of which tail is 2 ins
Feeds on insects
Young: one baby

Northern Grasshopper Mouse

A Northern Grasshopper Mouse is stouter than most other mice, and has a shorter tail. Its fur is grayish or pinkish cinnamon, and the tip of its tail is white. The Northern Grasshopper Mouse is found in dry prairies as well as in the desert, but it is most active on moonless nights. You might hear it—it stands on its back legs and whistles so loudly and shrilly that it can be heard over 100 yards away. It usually lives in the burrow of a ground squirrel, prairie dog or pocket gopher.

Rodent
Length: 5–7½ ins, of which tail is 1–2 ins

Feeds mostly on grasshoppers, and other insects, small mice, scorpions and some plants
Tracks: 4 toes on front, 5 toes on hind feet
Young: 2–3 litters, each with 2–6 babies

Insectivore
Length: 3–3½ ins, of which tail is about 1 ins
Feeds on insects
Tracks: 5 toes
Young: 2 litters, each with up to 6 babies

Desert Shrew

Like other shrews, Desert Shrews have long noses and small, beady eyes. Their fur is gray, and their ears are larger than those of other shrews. They are found in Southwest U.S. and in Mexico. Look for them where there are sagebrushes and prickly pear, or in garbage dumps where they hunt for food. Look for their nests beneath agave plants or under boards or debris, made with fine plant stems and sometimes with hair.

Pygmy Rabbit

Pygmy Rabbits are the smallest rabbits in North America, and the only ones to dig a burrow. You can tell it from similar-looking animals by its size. It is smaller than an Eastern Cottontail Rabbit (see page 18), and larger than a Pika (see page 54). It does not have a white tail like a Cottontail but, unlike a Pika, it does have a rabbit's long ears. Look for it where there is plenty of sagebrush and greasewood, and also in sand dunes. Although it is most active at night, you may see it during the day. Its simple burrow has two or more entrances.

Rabbit and Hare family
Length: 10–11 ins, of which tail is less than 1 ins
Feeds mainly on sagebrush
Tracks: 4 toes on front, 5 toes on hind feet, which are much longer
Young: one litter of 5–8 babies

White-tailed Antelope Squirrel

With its grayish fur, a White-tailed Antelope Squirrel is well camouflaged in the desert, except that it usually runs with its tail held tightly over its back, allowing the tail's white underside to flash in the sun. It looks similar to a chipmunk (see page 17), but is paler and a chipmunk does not have a white undertail. Antelope Squirrels do not need to drink because they get all the moisture they need from their food. They can be seen among rock crevices or peeking out of their burrows all day. They bounce as they move. The young are born underground in a nest lined with feathers, fur, and plant fibers.

Rodent – Length: 7½–9 ins, of which tail is 2–3 ins
Feeds on the seeds of cacti, yucca, and other
desert plants, and on insects
Tracks: 4 toes on front, 5 toes on hind feet
Young: one litter of 5–14 babies

Antelope Jack Rabbit

Antelope Jack Rabbits are large hares with long legs and ears up to 7½ ins long. You are most likely to notice their white undertail flashing through the cacti as they bound away. They are active from early in the evening until after dawn. During the day they rest in the shade of a bush, then groups of twenty or more move off to feed. They do not dig burrows, but the mother makes a nest in the ground or in a hollow cactus and lines it with fur. Sometimes, she leaves each baby in a separate hiding place.

Rabbit and Hare family
Length: 21–26 ins, of which tail is 2–3 ins
Feeds on grasses, mesquite, cacti, and other desert plants
Tracks: 4 toes on front, 5 toes on hind feet,
which are much longer
Young: up to 7 litters, each with 1–5 babies

Collared Peccary

You can recognize a Collared Peccary by its snout and pig-like shape. Its fur is coarse and grizzled gray or black. Look for the collar of paler fur around its neck. You are most likely to see them in small bands of up to twenty-five animals in the morning or late afternoon. Look for them in chaparral, rocky canyons, and among scrub oaks as well as in the desert. The young have reddish fur with a black stripe down their backs. They are strong enough to follow their mother only a few days after birth.

Ungulate: Peccary family – Length: 3 ft, of which tail is 2 ins
Feeds on cacti, prickly pears, and other desert plants
Tracks: 2-toed hooves – Young: up to 5 babies (usually 2)

Tracking Deer

Deer are often quite easy to spot. There are many herds in national parks and you can often get quite close to them without them running off. Be careful in the fall, however, when they are rutting (or mating) because they can be very bad tempered then.

You may also see deer in forests or on mountains, as well as Bighorn Sheep and Mountain Goats. Watch for them on the skyline. Look for their tracks, droppings, and other signs that they are nearby.

Discarded antlers

All male deer that grow antlers shed them in either the spring or the fall. Three or four months later they have grown a new pair. Even in places where there are lots of deer you will be lucky to find a shed antler. If you do find one, look for the tooth marks on it. Deer nibble their old antlers to get the minerals in them. You can sometimes tell how old a male deer is from the size of his antlers.

While a deer's new set of antlers are growing they are covered by a furry skin called "velvet." It feeds them with blood and nerves. When the antlers are fully grown, the blood dries up and the deer rubs the velvet off on low branches, leaving shiny, bony antlers.

Signs left on trees

Deer will strip bark off trees to eat, as well as using the trunk to remove the velvet from their antlers. How high they strip the tree depends on the deer. Moose can strip bark up to 10 feet high and Elk up to 6 feet, but Mule Deer do not go much higher than 3 feet. Bighorn Sheep also bite into bark. Look for the tooth marks to tell them apart. Deer leave deep, vertical marks, while sheep make slanting marks. Squirrels and small mammals leave much smaller tooth marks.

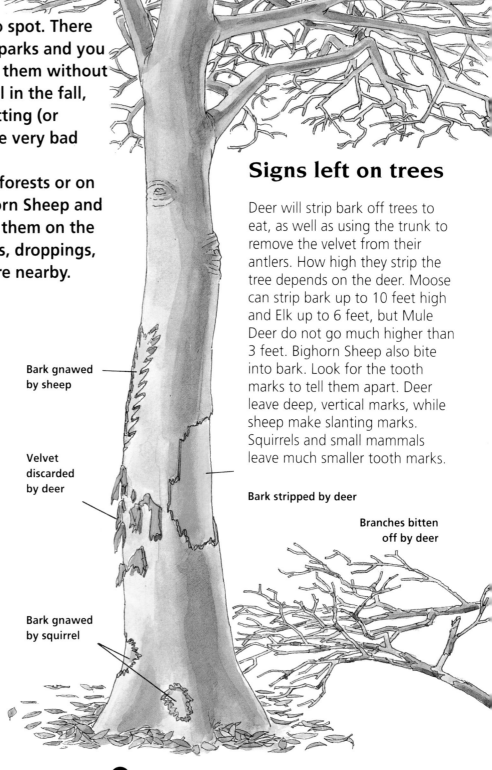

Bark gnawed by sheep

Velvet discarded by deer

Bark gnawed by squirrel

Bark stripped by deer

Branches bitten off by deer

Making a plaster cast

1 **Bend a strip of stiff card into a ring** a bit bigger than the footprint and fasten it with a paper-clip.
2 **Clear away any leaves or twigs** from the print and push the card into the ground so that the print is in the middle.
3 **Half fill a yogurt cup** with plaster of Paris and mix with water to make a thick paste.
4 **Pour the paste into the ring** all over the print and leave to set for about 30 minutes.
5 **Slide a knife under the cast** and lift it gently.
6 **Remove the card and clean** the mud off the cast with a nailbrush and water.

Footprints in the mud

If you find some clear prints in soft mud or snow, draw them in your notebook. If the prints have cloven hooves, you will know they have been made by a deer, cow, goat, or sheep.

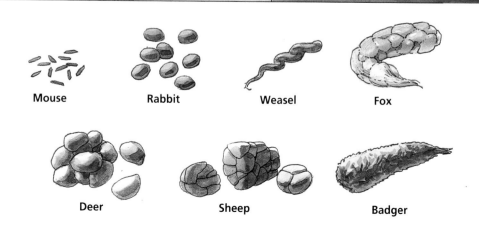

Droppings

Whatever the weather, animals always leave droppings, and they are one of the best ways of telling which animals are around. Look at the size, shape, and color to tell them apart, but do not touch them. Meat-eaters' droppings are usually long and contain undigested bits of animals. Plant-eaters' droppings are usually round or oval and contain plant fibers.

Mouse   Rabbit   Weasel   Fox

Deer   Sheep   Badger

Mountains & Tundra

The Rocky Mountains are the highest and longest range in North America. Further west are the Sierra Nevada and the Cascade Mountains, and in the East are the Appalachian Mountains. In the far north, the tundra lies between the Arctic snows and the coniferous forests. Living on the tundra is very similar to mountain living.

In winter, mountains and tundra are covered with a thick blanket of snow for several months. Icy winds sweep across the ground so that only a few small, tough plants can survive there. Many animals migrate to avoid the harshest weather. Caribou move south into the forests, while some mountain sheep and goats move lower down the slopes. Smaller mammals, such as marmots, hibernate in the winter or carry on living under the snow.

The climate is so harsh that the number of some mammals varies considerably from year to year. In very cold winters many animals, particularly small rodents, die. The animals that feed on them are affected too. Arctic foxes prey on lemmings and other rodents, so when there are fewer lemmings, there are fewer foxes too.

Most of the mammals have thick fur to protect them from the cold. Unfortunately, they have been much hunted for their beautiful fur. Some are now rare and in danger of extinction. The picture shows eight mammals from this book. How many can you recognize?

Grizzly Bear, Caribou (herd in distance), Moose, Arctic Fox, Mountain Goat, Hoary Marmot, Musk Ox, Bighorn Sheep.

Mountains & Tundra

Hog-nosed Skunk

You can tell this is a skunk from its black and white fur and bushy tail. Unlike other skunks, its back and tail are completely white. It gets the name "Hog-nosed" from its long, pig-like snout and, like pigs, it uses it to root in the ground for much of its food. It is most active at night, and during the day you can look for patches of ground it has "plowed" up in search of grubs. Hog-nosed Skunks live mostly in the foothills of Southwest U.S. They like partly wooded and rocky areas far away from humans. They live on their own, and make a den in a cleft in the rocks. Like other skunks, they defend themselves by spraying a foul scent at their attackers.

Carnivore: Weasel family
Length: 20–26 ins, of which tail is 7½–11½ ins
Feeds on insects, reptiles, spiders, plants, and small mammals
Tracks: 5 toes with pad
Young: one litter of 3–4 babies

Ringtail

A Ringtail looks a bit like a cat with its large ears and big eyes. Its fur is grayish above and buff below. You cannot miss its long tail with black and white rings. Racoons have similar tails, but are much larger, and have black and white face markings. Ringtails are secretive animals—they are most active at night and keep out of sight. They like dry, rocky places with cliffs and canyons, or woody places near water. They do not often leave tracks. They make their den in caves, rock crevices, and hollow trees. When Ringtails are cornered they release a foul smell from a gland under their tail.

Carnivore: Ringtail family
Length: 2–2½ ft, of which tail is about half
Feeds on small mammals, crickets, grasshoppers, scorpions, reptiles, fruit, and berries
Tracks: 5 toes
Young: one litter of 2–4 babies

Wolverine

Carnivore: Weasel family
Length: 2½–3½ft, of which tail is 6½–10 ins
Feeds on berries, shoots, and any animal it can catch
Tracks: 5-toed paw prints – Young: a litter of 2–5 babies

This animal is the largest member of the Weasel family, and looks like a small bear. Its shaggy coat is very dark brown with paler patches across its forehead and down its sides. It has large feet and thick legs. Wolverines live mainly in the Arctic, and are found across Alaska and northern Canada, and south through the Rockies. They live on their own, and are active day and night. They may travel many miles scavenging for food, and can smell carrion (dead animals) even under several feet of snow. They rob traps and are known to steal from trappers' food stores. Their powerful jaws can crunch through the bones of large animals such as Moose. They do not make a permanent burrow, but lay up during the day in any sheltered place they find.

Black Bear

Bears are the largest carnivores (meat-eaters) in the world. They have small, rounded ears, and their short tails are hidden among their thick fur. Black Bears are found over most of Canada, south into the Rockies to Mexico, and along the East Coast to Florida. Their fur is blackish in the East, but often a cinnamon brown in the West, where they may be confused with a Grizzly Bear (see right). They live on their own and hunt mainly at night, but they leave plenty of signs behind them. Look for mammal burrows that have been dug up, or strips of bark bitten or pulled off pine, spruce or fir trees. Young Black Bears sometimes climb aspen trees, leaving their claw marks in the bark. Bears also like to rub themselves against a favorite tree—look for bits of hair stuck to the bark. Black Bears hibernate in their dens made in a hollow tree or beneath roots.

Carnivore: Bear family
Length: 4 1/2–6 ft, of which tail is 3–6 ins
Feeds on almost everything,
including insects, small mammals,
berries, leaves, carrion, fish, and honey
Tracks: 5 toes with pad
Young: one litter of 1–5 cubs

Grizzly Bear

Grizzly Bears get their name from the white tips to their brownish or yellowish fur. They are easily annoyed and can be very dangerous if disturbed, particularly when they are with their cubs. They live in the wild mainly in Alaska and Northwest Canada, but are still found in the Rockies as far south as Yellowstone National Park. If you are camping in the park, keep your food store outside your tent, so if a Grizzly comes to raid it, you will not meet it face to face! If you are in bear country, it is important to be able to recognize any signs that Grizzlies are about. Look for their droppings and tracks, for bark ripped off trees, and for bear hairs stuck to bark. Grizzly Bears live on their own, and make a den in a cave or among tree roots. They hunt mostly at dawn and dusk, but you may come across one at other times, too. They hide uneaten carcasses, sometimes by lying on top of them for two to three weeks. If you find a carcass, get away from it. The Grizzly will not be far away and will attack to defend its food supply.

Carnivore: Bear family
Length: 6–7 ft of which tail is only 3 ins
Feeds on meat, fruit, grubs, fish, and anything it can find
Tracks: 5 toes
Young: a litter of 1–4 cubs, every second year

Mountains & Tundra

Pika

Pikas look very like guinea pigs, but have larger, furry ears. They are also called Rock Rabbits, but their ears are much smaller than those of a rabbit and Pikas have no tail. They live in large colonies among rocky screes, high in the mountains from British Columbia south to California and New Mexico. Listen out for their strange, short whistles. They collect piles of plants and leave them to dry in haystacks among the rocks, before taking them underground to their dens. If you see a pile of fresh hay, look among the rocks around you. You may well see a Pika hunched up and camouflaged on a boulder. Watch it hop to its den deep among the rocks. Look too for their black, sticky droppings.

Pika family
Length: 7 ins
Feeds on a wide range of plants
Tracks: 4 toes on front,
5 toes on hind feet
Young: 1–2 litters, each with 1–6 babies

Nuttall's Cottontail

Rabbit and Hare family
Length: 13–16 ins, of which tail is 1–2 ins
Feeds on grasses, sagebrush, juniper, and other woody shrubs
Tracks: 4 toes on front, 5 toes on hind feet which are much longer
Young: 3–5 litters, each with 1–8 babies

This is the Cottontail you are most likely to see in the Rockies from the Canadian border south to New Mexico. It is also known as the Mountain Cottontail. It is grayish brown above and white below. Look for its large, grizzled tail. Its ears are shorter than those of many other rabbits. It feeds mostly in the early evening and during the morning. During the day, it lays up in a hollow in the ground, among the rocks or in an underground burrow.

Sagebrush Vole

Rodent
Length: 4¹⁄₂–5¹⁄₂ ins, of which tail is ¹⁄₂–1 ins
Feeds on the leaves and woody parts of sagebrush
Tracks: 4 toes on front, 5 toes on hind feet
Young: usually more than 1 litter, each with 3–6 babies

Look for this small vole among sagebrush steppes and dry prairies in the Rockies from Washington south to eastern California. It is pale gray above and whitish below, and is the only vole you are likely to see here. It is active day and night, and builds its nest under shrubs. Look for the shallow tunnels it makes from its nest to nearby shrubs. Sagebrush Voles live in loose colonies, so if you see one animal, look around for signs of others, too.

Eastern Wood Rat

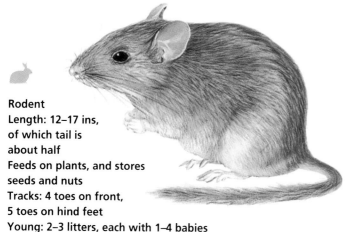

Rodent
Length: 12–17 ins,
of which tail is
about half
Feeds on plants, and stores
seeds and nuts
Tracks: 4 toes on front,
5 toes on hind feet
Young: 2–3 litters, each with 1–4 babies

Eastern Wood Rats look like Brown Rats (see page 14), but their tails are furry and their ears are larger. They are gray-brown above and white below, and are found in most of the eastern U.S., but not north of North Carolina. They are most active at night, so you will be lucky to see these animals, but you will certainly see their houses. Look for large piles of twigs, sticks, and leaves decorated with bottle tops, gun shells, and other bright objects. (On the Plains they build houses up to 4 ft across and almost as high.) They build their houses over their nests, which may be dug underground or made in a crack of a rock or in a hollow tree. You will soon notice the distinctive smell of their dens.

Hoary Marmot

Hoary Marmots are usually found higher up in the mountains and farther north than Yellow-bellied Marmots. It is sometimes called the Mountain Marmot. Their fur is mostly silvery gray. Look for their black and white faces among the stones of a rockslide and for the large mounds of dirt which show where their burrows are. Listen out for their shrill warning whistle. They feed during the day, but hibernate from October to February.

Rodent
Length: 24–30 ins, of which tail is 6½–9½ ins
Feeds mostly on grass and green leaves
Tracks: 4 toes on front, 5 toes on hind feet
Young: one litter of 4–5 babies

Yellow-bellied Marmot

The Yellow-bellied Marmot is yellowish brown above and, as its name implies, has a yellowish belly. It has a heavy body and a longish tail. You may see it on rocky hillsides of the Rockies, the Cascades, and the Sierras. It feeds during the day, and makes its den among rock piles or in a burrow. The entrance to the den is usually near a large boulder, which it uses as a lookout post. Listen out for its high-pitched chirp which warns other marmots of danger.

Rodent
Length: 18–27 ins, of which tail is 5–8½ ins
Feeds on green plants, such as grasses and lupines
Tracks: 4 toes on front, 5 toes on hind feet
Young: one litter of about 5 babies

Mountains & Tundra

Elk

At one time Elk roamed over much of North America, but now there are only a scattered few outside the Rockies. They are reddish brown with a yellowish rump and tail. You are most likely to see Elk in a forest in a group of up to twenty-five animals. You can easily tell the stags (males), from the hinds (females). Stags are larger and have shaggy hair around their neck. In late summer and fall, they have large, branching antlers. Listen out for the stag's bugle-like call as he defends his group of females from other males. Males shed their antlers in February or March and the Elk move higher up the mountains in spring.

Ungulate
Length 6½–9½ ft, of which tail is 2½–6½ ins
Feeds on grasses and shrubs
Tracks: 2-toed hooves
Young: usually a single calf, sometimes twins

Mountain Goat

You cannot mistake a Mountain Goat, with its shaggy white fur, white beard, and black eyes, nose, horns, and hooves, but you will have to climb high up the mountains to see it. Look for it on rocky crags near the snowline. It is found in the Rockies from Alaska south to Montana and Idaho, and has been introduced into nearby states as well. Unlike deer, Mountain Goats have horns that never branch and are never shed. Both males and females have them. A Mountain Goat is a superb climber and often makes its bed on a rocky ledge. Its droppings look like those of deer or sheep.

Ungulate
Length: 4–5½ ft, of which tail is 3½–8 ins
Feeds on grasses, shrubs, and other plants
Tracks: 2-toed hooves
Young: one kid

Bighorn Sheep

You may see Bighorn Sheep not only in the foothills and on the meadows of the mountains, but also in the prairies and deserts from Alberta to Mexico. They are usually brown above and paler below, although in the desert they are paler all over. The rams (males) have huge, coiled horns. The ewes (females) are smaller than the rams and their horns do not coil. Bighorns live together in herds of up to 100 animals, although males and females usually live apart in summer. During the mating season, the males compete with each other for females, and then you can hear their horns clashing up to a mile away. Look for their "beds" on rocky outposts—they scrape the ground to make a shallow dip then lie down. A Bighorn Sheep will return to the same bed again and again, so there is always a lot of dung nearby.

Ungulate
Length: 5–6 ft, of which tail is 3–5 ins
Feeds on grasses, sedges, bushes, and other plants, including cacti
Tracks: 2-toed hooves
Young: one lamb, sometimes twins

Barbary Sheep

Barbary Sheep have been introduced into North America from North Africa, and are probably more common here than in Africa. They are tawny brown and have a long beard. Notice how their horns bend outward. You can see them in dry canyons and on rocky hillsides in the southwest U.S. and Mexico. They do not need to drink water because they get enough moisture from dew and the plants they eat.

Ungulate
Length: 4–6 ft, of which tail is 9 ins
Feeds on grasses, shrubs, and crops
Tracks: 2-toed hooves
Young: 1–3 lambs

Mountains & Tundra

Arctic Fox

Arctic Foxes vary in color: in summer, they are brown or grayish white, while in winter they are white or slate blue with a brownish head and feet. Arctic Foxes are slightly smaller than Red Foxes (see page 13), and have smaller ears and bushier tails. They live in Alaska and northern Canada, and their feet are heavily covered with fur to protect them from the cold. They are not shy of humans, and come close to the homes of people. They follow Polar Bears in winter, hoping to feed on the carrion they leave behind. They make a den on a well-drained slope and do not roam far from it until the cubs are old enough to take care of themselves. They are usually silent, although they can bark, howl, yelp, and wail. The warning cries of birds are the most likely sign that an Arctic Fox is about.

Carnivore: Dog family
Length: 2½–3 ft, of which tail is about a third
Feeds mainly on voles, lemmings, nesting birds, and carrion left by Polar Bears
Tracks: 4-toed paw prints
Young: one litter, usually of 5–6 cubs

Polar Bear

You cannot mistake a Polar Bear—if you see one in a zoo, notice its big feet and small ears. You would have to go right up to the Arctic to see one in the wild. It keeps to the icy coasts, and lives on its own, wandering across the pack ice in search of food. It is an excellent swimmer. It usually walks very slowly, with its head down and swinging from side to side. In winter, the females give birth to their cubs in dens dug in snowdrifts. They stay there until the weather becomes warmer and the cubs are large enough to leave.

Carnivore: Bear family
Length: 7–8 ft, of which only 3–5 ins is tail
Feeds mainly on Ringed Seals, whale carcasses, birds, berries, and grass
Tracks: 5 toes
Young: 1–3 cubs, every 2–4 years

Caribou

Caribou are also known as Reindeer. Their fur is brownish and shaggy, with paler underparts, neck, and rump. Both males and females carry antlers, although the females' are smaller than the males'. Their wide hooves stop them sinking into the snow. They are found across the far north from Alaska to Newfoundland, and south into the Rockies. They form large herds of up to 100,000 animals, and are always on the move. In the rutting season, the bulls (males) gather harems of twelve to fifteen cows (females). The calves are born between May and July, and are strong enough to follow the herd even before they are a day old. Inuits and trappers hunt Caribou, not just for their meat, but also for their skins.

Ungulate: Deer family
Length: 4¹/₂–6¹/₂ ft, of which tail is 4–7¹/₂ ins
Feeds on lichens, twigs, sedges, and fungi
Tracks: 2-toed rounded hooves
Young: 1, sometimes 2, calves

Musk Ox

You cannot mistake a Musk Ox with its hunched shoulders and long, dark hair which, in winter, reaches almost to the ground. Notice how its horns grow from a central base down each side of its face. You are most likely to see Musk Oxen in zoos, although they still live in the wild in the extreme north of Arctic Canada. In winter, they are most likely to be seen on windswept hilltops where the snow has been blown away. They are active both day and night. In summer, Musk Oxen form small groups of up to twelve animals, and these join together to form larger herds in winter. If they are threatened, the adults form a defensive circle, each with their horns facing outward, and with the young calves protected in the center.

Ungulate
Length: 6–8 ft, of which tail is 2¹/₂–6¹/₂ ins
Feeds on lichens, grasses, sedges, and other tundra plants
Tracks: 2-toed circular hooves
Young: 1 calf every other year

Rivers & Waterways

The animals in this section all live in or near fresh water. Some live among the sedges, reeds, and rushes that grow beside lakes, ponds, rivers, streams, and marshes. Look for their burrows in the banks.

Otters, mink, and beavers are well adapted to living in water, but have to come to the surface to breathe. Their soft, thick fur keeps them warm and is protected by a layer of longer, waterproof, "guard" hairs.

Beavers like to live in swampy areas. They use twigs and branches filled with mud to build a dam across a stream and so make their own swamps, which alter the landscape. In most places, however, they are now protected and controlled so that they are again becoming more widespread. The picture shows seven mammals from this book. How many can you recognize?

Beaver, Mink, Muskrat, Nutria, River Otter, Swamp Rabbit, Water Shrew.

Marsh Rice Rat

This Rice Rat is very common in the southeastern U.S. as far north as New Jersey, but, since it is most active at night, you will rarely see it. It is grayish-brown above and paler below. It is smaller than a Brown Rat (see page 14), and has a longer tail. It lives in salt marshes and areas with sedges and grasses. It lives partly in water and partly on land, and builds a nest with grass and sedge in low bushes or rushes, or under debris. It also makes runways through the grass, and digs underground tunnels.

Rodent
Length: 7½–12 ins, of which half is the tail
Feeds on grains, seeds, plants, insects, and small crabs
Tracks:
4 toes on front, 5 toes on back feet
Young: several litters a year, each with 1–5 young

Mink

You can tell that a Mink belongs to the weasel family by its long body, short legs, small head, and long tail. It is larger than most other weasels, though smaller than the Pine Marten and the Fisher (see page 27). It has glossy, dark brown, almost black, fur. It is found over much of Canada and the U.S., except in the deserts of the Southwest. Look for it in marshes, swamps, ponds, lakes, and rivers. It is an excellent swimmer and, in winter, it can swim under the ice, breathing from pockets of trapped air. It is most active at night, and lives on its own. Look for its den, which it digs into the bank of a stream or lake, and for its tracks in soft mud.

Carnivore: Weasel family
Length: 18–28 ins, of which tail is about a third
Feeds on a wide variety of animals
Tracks: 5 toes – Young: one litter of 1–8 babies

River Otter

River Otters are quite like Minks. However, its sleek fur is mid-brown and shorter than a Mink's. It has webbed feet, and its long tail starts off broad and tapers to a point. Look for River Otters at the coast and in estuaries, as well as near lakes and streams. Sometimes they travel overland to get from one stream or lake to another. They often travel in pairs or family groups, and are mainly active at night. They swim and dive through the water, and play on the riverbank. Look for slides in the mud or snow down to the water. They dig dens among the roots of shrubs or in holes in the riverbank.

Carnivore: Weasel family
Length: 3–4 ft, of which tail is 12–19 ins
Feeds on fish, water birds, small mammals, frogs, and shellfish
Tracks: 5 toes
Young: one litter of 1–6 babies

Rivers & Waterways

Water Shrew

Insectivore
Length: 5–6½ ins, of which tail is up to 3½ ins
Feeds on earthworms, mayfly nymphs, and other
small water creatures
Tracks: 5 toes
Young: more than 1 litter, each with up to 8 babies

Water Shrews are smaller than Rice Rats and have darker fur. Their small ears are almost completely hidden in their fur. They are found throughout much of Canada and the U.S., except in the Southeast and the Plains. Look for them in marshes, streams, and rivers where there are plenty of trees. They are extremely active, swimming and diving in the water. As they dive, their fur traps bubbles of air, so they seem to be covered in a silvery film. They can also run across the surface of the water. They make a nest of dried twigs, bark, and leaves among the plants and roots on the riverbank.

Swamp Rabbit

Swamp Rabbits are the largest cottontails. Their fur is yellow brown, mottled with black on top and white below. Their tail is thin and slender and white underneath. Look for them in swamps and other wet ground in the southern U.S., from eastern Texas and Oklahoma to Georgia. Swamp Rabbits are quite at home in water and swim well. They do not dig burrows, but make their nests under logs or in hollows in the ground. Sometimes they hide under water with only their noses above the surface. Look for their droppings left on logs.

Rabbit and Hare family
Length: 18–21 ins,
of which tail is 2½ ins
Feeds on plants,
including water
plants and crops
Tracks: 4 toes on
front, 5 toes on
back feet which are much longer
Young: 2 litters, each with 1–5 babies

Muskrat

A Muskrat can be confused with a Beaver, but it is smaller and its tail is much narrower and flattened from side to side. It sometimes lives close to Beavers, but normally builds its own similar-looking, but smaller lodge of grasses and sedges. It uses its lodge as a place to shelter and keep warm. Or it digs a burrow into the bank which can be used by Muskrats for up to thirty years and may have several different chambers. Muskrats are found all over North America, except in the desert, the permanently frozen land of the Arctic, Florida, and Georgia. Wherever there is water and cattails, you are likely to see muskrats, even in cities. They like to feed on a flattened platform of vegetation, and here you can see the remains of their food.

Rodent – **Length: 16–25 ins, of which tail is 7–11½ ins**
Feeds mostly on water plants, but also clams, frogs, and fish
Tracks: 5 toes
Young: 1–5 litters, each
with 1–11 babies

Nutria

Nutrias are also known as Coypus. They were introduced into Louisiana from South America, and have now spread into swamps, marshes, ponds, and canals in surrounding states, and into Oregon and other Northwest states. To tell them apart from Beavers and Muskrats, look at their tails. A Beaver's tail is flattened into a paddle, a Muskrat's is flattened vertically, while a Nutria's is long and rounded. It is most active at night, and carries its food to a feeding station, which may be a log, brush or other plants strong enough to hold the animal. It digs a burrow into the riverbank and often damages the sides of canals and streams. It is considered a pest in some areas, as it feeds on crops.

Rodent
Length: 2–4¹/₂ ft, of which tail is 10–17 ins
Feeds on plants, both land and water
Tracks: 5-toed webbed feet
Young: one litter of 2–11 babies

Beaver

A Beaver is large with dark blackish brown fur and a broad, flat tail, shaped like a paddle which helps it to swim through the water. Listen out for a loud crack as its slaps its tail on the water before diving. Beavers used to be found in wetlands right across North America, but are now rare in many areas, particularly in Florida and California. The best places to see them are in the northern national parks and refuges. They are most active at night, but are sometimes seen during the day. Look for their dam built of mud and sticks across a stream or for their conical lodge built on the edge of a lake. Look too for the stumps of small trees which they have bitten through with their long front teeth and dragged to their home.

Rodent
Length: 3–4 ft, of which tail is 12–17 ins
Feeds on twigs and leaves
Tracks: 5-toed webbed feet
Young: one litter of 1–8 babies

Detecting Rodents

Field voles, jumping mice, and harvest mice may be too fast and small for you to see, but you can look for their discarded food, runways, and nest holes. They are also a food source for other animals. You may find their bones in an empty, discarded bottle, or in an owl pellet.

Looking for tooth marks

Rodents have two large front teeth which never stop growing. They do not get too large because they are constantly worn away as the animal chews. The next time you go walking in the countryside or in a park, look for chewed nuts and pine cones. Look for chewed bark and roots of trees as well. Beavers sometimes gnaw right through tree trunks.

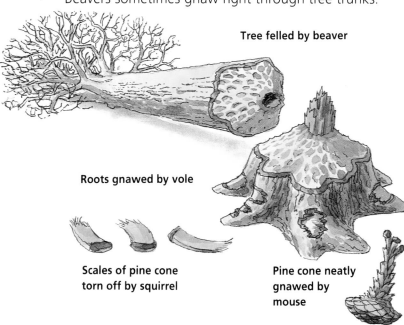

Tree felled by beaver

Roots gnawed by vole

Scales of pine cone torn off by squirrel

Pine cone neatly gnawed by mouse

Walnut shell gnawed by vole

Walnut shell gnawed by mouse

Walnut shell gnawed by squirrel

Winter home for harvest mice

If you live in the country, you may find harvest mice creeping into your garden to make a nest for the winter. Encourage them to come by providing a good home for them.

1 **Ask an adult to cut a slice off one side of an old tennis ball.**

Tunnels and runways

Most mammals follow a regular route as they hunt. Mice, voles, and shrews make runways through fallen leaves and among the grass. If you can follow them, they may lead to their nest. Look, too, for tunnels leading into the soft soil of riverbanks. If a hole is less than 2 inches across, you can be sure it was made by a small rodent.

Moles stay under ground, but you can see the spoil hole by clearing away the soil from a mole hill. Don't worry, you will not disturb the mole—it is much faster than you.

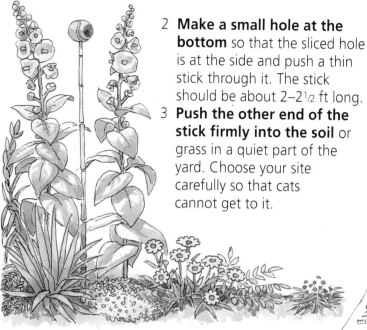

2 **Make a small hole at the bottom** so that the sliced hole is at the side and push a thin stick through it. The stick should be about 2–2½ ft long.

3 **Push the other end of the stick firmly into the soil** or grass in a quiet part of the yard. Choose your site carefully so that cats cannot get to it.

Dissecting an owl pellet

Owls swallow their prey whole, but they cough up the parts they cannot digest in the form of a pellet. If you find an owl pellet—look under their roosts and feeding perches— put it in a plastic bag and take it home to examine it.

1 **Soak the pellet for about an hour** in a bowl of warm water.

Attracting mammals

If you think there are mice or squirrels nearby and you want them to come into your garden, try leaving out food for them, like nuts, seeds, bits of carrot, or bread soaked in water. **Be careful though**, you may attract rats and they carry disease. If you do see a rat (see page 15), clear your garden of food, and get an adult to inform the Pest Control Officer or local health officials.

2 **When the pellet is soft, put it on an old newspaper** and gently pull it apart with tweezers, a large nail, or a small screwdriver.

3 **Lay out the bones**. Can you tell which bones they are? If you find teeth attached to a bone, it must be a piece of jawbone.

4 **Wash your hands with soap and water.**

Mice, squirrels and birds will like this food.

Cats, gophers, badgers and foxes will like this food.

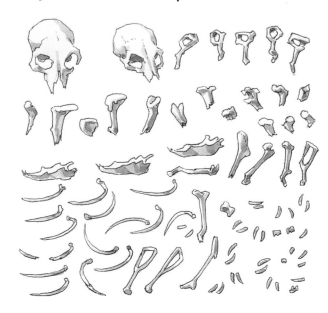

Coasts & Marine

The sea can be a harsh place to live, especially in winter when huge waves are whipped up by gales and storms. Some mammals go farther out to sea to find calmer water, while others come ashore or shelter in bays and harbors.

Apart from sea otters, most sea mammals have fins and flippers instead of legs. They swim under the water, but have to come to the surface to breathe air. They have little or no hair on their skin, but instead have a thick layer of fat, called "blubber," to keep them warm.

Seals, sea lions, and walruses come ashore to give birth and look after their young. They form huge breeding colonies and return to the same grounds year after year. If you go to see one, be careful not to disturb the animals. Seals sometimes come ashore to rest on rocks and sand banks.

Whales and dolphins stay farther out to sea and never leave the water. Many whales swim along the coasts of North America as they migrate between the Arctic and the tropics. If you are lucky enough to see a school of whales swimming through the water, "blowing" out their damp, hot plumes of air, it is a sight you will never forget.

Unfortunately, sea mammals are still not safe from hunters. Young seals are covered with a soft fur called "lanugo." In spite of public protest many are killed for their fur. Norway and Japan still kill many thousands of minke whales each year. This picture shows five mammals from this book. How many can you recognize?

Common Dolphins, Sea Otter, Northern Sea Lions, Gray Whale, Humpbacked Whale.

Coasts & Marine

Sea Otter

Look for Sea Otters on the Pacific Coast of North America, in the Aleutian Islands, Alaska, and as far south as Monterey, California. A Sea Otter spends almost all of its life at sea, resting and feeding among the kelp. Its feet are webbed and are more like flippers than feet. Look for its long tail to tell it apart from seals. It likes to swim on its back, when you will see its grayish head and neck. It breaks open sea urchins by smashing them against a rock held on its chest. It seldom comes ashore, except when there are severe storms. The pups are born at sea, and can swim on their own by the time they are two weeks old.

Carnivore:
Weasel family
Length: 2½–5½ ft
of which tail is
10–14 ins
Feeds on shellfish
and sea urchins
Young:
usually
one pup

Sea lions, walruses and seals all have flippers instead of front and back legs. They have streamlined bodies and are well adapted to swimming, but like all sea mammals, they have to come to the surface to breathe in air. Watch for their heads bobbing up out of the water. They haul themselves on to land, both to rest and to breed, and this is the best time to see them.

Northern Sea Lion

You can tell a Fur Seal or a sea lion from a seal or Walrus because you can see its ears. Seals and Walruses can hear too, but only a hole in their skin shows where their ears are. The Northern Sea Lion is common in the Pacific from California to Alaska. It is brownish or sometimes yellowish in color, and the bulls (males) are about three times as heavy as cows. Soon after the pups are born, the bulls gather together a harem (breeding group) of about twenty to thirty cows to breed again. If you see a sea lion at the zoo, notice how it turns its back flippers forward to help it walk on land.

Sea mammal: Sea Lion family
Length: about 9 ft
Feeds on fish and squid
Young: one pup

Californian Sea Lion

Californian Sea Lions are the most familiar sea lions and the ones you are most likely to see at aquaria. Listen out for their constant, loud barking. Even in the wild they like to play and seem to be performing. Look for them on the Pacific Coast from Vancouver south to Baja California. A Californian Sea Lion is darker than the Northern Sea Lion. Look for their large eyes and small, pointed ears. They spend most of their time at sea, but are sometimes seen on rocky beaches. They are very sociable and gather in large colonies to breed. Each bull gathers a harem of cows.

Sea mammal:
Sea Lion family
Length: about 8 ft
(female much smaller)
Feeds on fish,
squid, octopus,
abalone, and rock fish
Young: one pup

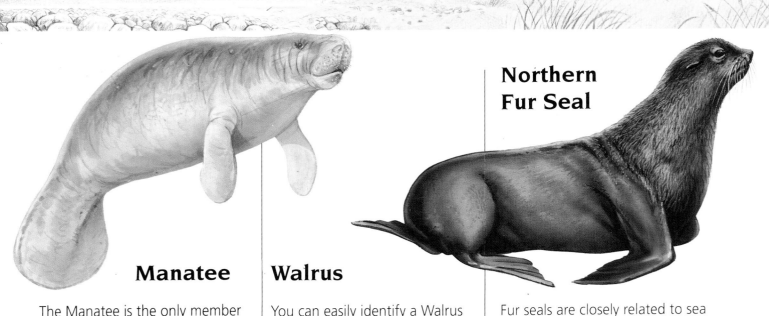

Manatee

The Manatee is the only member of its family. It likes warm waters, and is found in estuaries and inlets from the Caribbean as far north as Florida and the Carolinas. Look for its broad head and thick lips. Only the front part can be seen out of the water, but you may see the rest of it in clear, shallow water. Look then for its broad, flattened tail. It has front flippers only and these are broad too, like paddles. It moves very slowly, and cannot dive fast enough to escape danger—many have been killed or maimed by the propellers of power boats. They never leave the water, even to have their pups.

Sea mammal: Manatee family
Length: about 15 ft
Feeds on water plants
Young: one pup every 2–3 years

Walrus

You can easily identify a Walrus from its long tusks—the largest bulls have tusks up to 3 ft long. It uses them to scrape shellfish off the seabed and to haul itself on to the ice. Walruses are found in the Arctic on both the Atlantic and Pacific Coasts, but those in the West are larger than those in the East (they are sometimes found farther south). They are usually seen in groups along the edge of the ice pack.

Sea mammal: Walrus family
Length: about 11½ ft
Feeds on shellfish gathered from the seabed
Young: one pup every second year

Northern Fur Seal

Fur seals are closely related to sea lions and, like them, have visible external ears. They have long whiskers and a pointed snout. Males are blackish above and reddish below. Females are much smaller and grayer. Northern Fur Seals spend between six and eight months at sea. They can dive to a depth of 180 ft to catch fish and squid, and swim up to 6,200 miles to their breeding grounds in the Bering Sea. Many die accidentally from oil spills, and from swallowing plastic bands and polythene bags.

Sea mammal: Sea Lion family
Length: about 8 ft
Feeds on fish, squid, and cuttlefish
Young: one pup

Coasts & Marine

Unlike sea lions and walruses, seals cannot turn their back flippers forward to help them walk on land. Instead, they have to wriggle over the ground.

Ribbon Seal

Sea mammal: Seal family – Length: about 5½ ft
Feeds on fish and squid – Young: one pup

Ribbon Seals are rare, but if you saw one you would identify it quite easily from the bands of yellowish white around its neck, front flippers, and rump. The rest of its fur is dark brown. It breeds only in the Arctic, and comes no farther south than the drifting ice pack and the Alaskan Peninsula. It climbs up on to drifting ice to breed. Its pup is born on the ice in spring, and is covered with white fur.

In North America, Harp Seals are found only in the Atlantic waters of the Arctic, as far south as Hudson's Bay and the Gulf of St. Lawrence. The bulls are creamy white or grayish with a black mark across their backs more or less in the shape of a harp. The cows are not so clearly marked. Harp Seals can dive up to 600 ft in search of food and may swim many miles. However, they always keep fairly close to pack ice, and the young are born on the ice in February or March. There are many fewer Harp Seals than there used to be. They are still hunted; the skins of both pups and adults are used for clothing and leather.

Harp Seal

Sea mammal: Seal family
Length: about 6½ ft
Feeds mostly on fish and shellfish
Young: one pup

Hooded Seal

Sea mammal: Seal family – Length: about 8 ft
Feeds on fish and squid – Young: one pup

Hooded Seals get their name from a bag of skin on top of their heads, which the bull can inflate like a hood when he is angry, to make him look more fierce. Hooded Seals are grayish with brown and cream blotches. They live on the Atlantic side of the Arctic, and are found between Baffin Island and the Gulf of St. Lawrence, but not in Hudson's Bay. A bull mates with only one cow. The pup is born on ice toward the end of March.

Ringed Seal

This small seal looks rather like a Harbor Seal, but has white rings as well as dark spots on its gray back. It has brown whiskers and a cat-like face. It is the most common seal in the Arctic, and comes as far south as Labrador, Newfoundland, Hudson's Bay, and Point Barrow in Alaska. When the sea is frozen over, it digs breathing holes in the ice with its flippers. Ringed seals live more or less on their own, except when they are breeding. When a cow is ready to give birth, she digs a large den for herself and her pup in a snow drift. After the pup is born, she will sometimes move it from den to den to avoid predators.

Sea mammal: Seal family
Length: about 5 ft
Feeds on small fish, shellfish, and shrimps – Young: one pup

Harbor Seal

Harbor Seals have a short, round head with a definite forehead, rather like a dog's. They vary in color, but are usually bluish gray above with many dark blotches and streaks. You may see them close to the coast, in harbors, and in river estuaries on both the East and West Coasts of North America. They come ashore to give birth, usually in early summer. The pup takes to the water often after only a few hours or a day or two.

Sea mammal: Seal family
Length: about 5½ ft
Feeds mainly on fish,
but also takes shellfish
Young: usually one pup

Northern Elephant Seal

This huge seal swims in the seas along the Pacific Coast from the Gulf of Alaska to Baja California. It gets its name from its large size and from its snout, which looks a bit like a trunk. They come ashore in December and January so the cows (females) can give birth to the pups. The bulls (males) come first and establish a territory for their own harem (group of cows). Look for them on sandy shores, where they lie very close together. You can easily tell which animals are the bulls. They are almost twice as big as the cows, and in the breeding season they inflate their snouts to make them look bigger. The pups are covered with black fur, and stay on land until they are about five months old.

Sea mammal:
Seal family
Length: bulls
about 20 ft,
cows 10–12 ft
Feeds on small
sharks, other fish,
and squid
Young: one pup

Coasts & Marine

Dolphins and whales live totally in the sea. They have no fur and their tails are horizontal, not vertical as with fish. Look for the notch in the middle of the tail. Like other sea mammals, they need to breathe air, which they do through blowholes on top of their head. Both dolphins and porpoises like to play across the bows of ships, and this is probably the best way to get a good look at them.

Harbor Porpoise

Harbor Porpoises are also known as Common Porpoises. They have no beak, and are smaller and stouter than most other dolphins. They are dark gray or black above and white below. You can see them on the Atlantic and Pacific Coasts. They usually travel in small groups of ten to fifteen animals. Look for them in shallow water near the coast and in estuaries, harbors, and rivers—watch for their black heads breaking the water to breathe. If you see one close to, look for the gray line from its jaws to its flippers.

Sea mammal: Dolphin family
Length: about 5 ft
Feeds on fish, shellfish, and squid
Young: one calf every 2 years

Short-finned Pilot Whale

This pilot whale is blackish all over, but the best way to recognize it is by its long, narrow flippers and bulging forehead. It may be seen on the Atlantic Coast, as far north as New England, and on the Pacific Coast up to Alaska. It usually swims in schools of up to 2,000 animals. In dolphinaria it can perform almost as well as Bottle-nosed Dolphins.

Sea mammal: Dolphin family
Length: about 22 ft
Feeds mainly on squid
Young: one calf every 3 years

Common Dolphin

Common Dolphins are smaller than many other dolphins and have a large "beak." They have black backs with white undersides and yellowish sides. They are very sociable and sometimes swim in groups of over 1,000 animals. They live in warm and temperate waters in both the Atlantic and Pacific Oceans, usually keeping some way out from land, but you can also see them at aquaria throughout North America. In the wild, they like to ride the bow waves of ships and leap high out of the water.

Sea mammal: Dolphin family
Length: about 8 ft
Feeds on fish, including flying fish
Young: one calf every 2–3 years

Pacific White-sided Dolphin

Pacific White-sided Dolphins have short, rounded snouts. Their backs are greenish black and, as their name suggests, they have white stripes down their sides. They are fast swimmers. Look for their dorsal fins cutting through the surface of the water. They swim close to the shore in winter, but farther out in summer. You may see them in large groups, often with seals and sea lions. They also like to ride the bow waves of ships. They are often seen in aquaria on the West Coast.

Sea mammal: Dolphin family
Length: about 7 ft
Feeds on fish and squid
Young: one calf

Bottle-nosed Dolphin

Sea mammal: Dolphin family
Length: about 13 ft
Feeds on fish from the seabed
Young: one calf every 2 years

Bottle-nosed Dolphins are bluish gray above and paler below. They have short beaks and jutting lower jaws. These are the dolphins most often used in dolphinaria. They are slow swimmers, and often leap clear out of the water. They swim in small groups, although they may form large schools of several thousands. They like to ride the bow waves of ships. They are the most common dolphin along the Atlantic Coast. You may see them in coastal lagoons, bays, and sometimes in rivers on the Pacific as well as on the Atlantic Coast.

Whales are related to dolphins, but have a much smaller dorsal fin. There are two kinds of whale: baleen whales that filter the water through baleen (horny plates that hang from the upper jaw) to catch their food, and toothed whales that can bite their food. As a whale breathes out, it blows a cloud of mist into the air. You can identify a whale from the shape of its blow. Some whales, like bats, use a form of echo location (see page 21) to help them detect rocks and other fish in the water. They emit a stream of clicks and listen for their echoes bouncing off objects near them.

Fin Whale

This is the second largest kind of whale after the Blue Whale. It is sometimes called the Common Rorqual, and is one of the rorquals most often seen. Fin Whales are shaped like torpedoes, are generally dark bluish gray, and their small dorsal fins are set well back. They swim fast and lift their head and blowhole out of the water to breathe. Then they blow one, tall spout of mist about 12–18 ft high, before diving again. Sometimes they leap clear out of the water, falling back with a loud, belly-flopping crash. Look for them swimming close to land in spring as they migrate from the warm waters of the South up to the cold, food-laden waters of the North. In fall, they swim south again.

Sea mammal: Baleen Whale – Length: about 78 ft
Feeds on plankton and fish
Young: one calf every 2–3 years

Blue Whale

Blue Whales are the largest animals that have ever lived, and they are now very rare. They have been hunted almost to extinction and, like many other whales, are now protected. Blue Whales are occasionally seen off the Atlantic and Pacific Coasts, and look very similar to Fin Whales. Their blow is almost vertical and may be as high as 20 ft. They spend the summer in the cold Arctic waters feeding, and move south to breed in warmer waters in the winter.

Sea mammal: Baleen Whale
Length: about 100 ft
Feeds on plankton
Young: one calf every 2–3 years

Minke Whale

The Minke Whale is the smallest rorqual. It is dark gray black, but paler underneath, and often has a white band on the upper side of its flippers. It blows out a low plume only about 6 ft high, which can be very hard to see. Minke Whales are found in both the Atlantic and Pacific oceans. They swim closer to the coast than other baleen whales, and are still hunted by Norwegian and Japanese whalers for "scientific research," in spite of a worldwide ban. Like many other whales, they feed in winter in the cold, northern oceans, and migrate south in summer to the tropics to breed. They sometimes leap out of the water, but dive back in headfirst with their tails arched.

Sea mammal: Baleen Whale
Length: up to 30 ft
Feeds on fish and plankton
Young: one calf every 2 years

Gray Whale

A Gray Whale has a narrow head and no fin on its back. When it blows, it makes a quick, low spout. Both Gray Whales and Humpback Whales are often covered with barnacles and whale lice. They rub themselves against underwater rocks to scrape the barnacles off. Like Humpback Whales, Gray Whales leap out of the water and are acrobatic swimmers. The best time to see them is between November and May. They breed in the waters around Baja California, then migrate to the northern Pacific and Arctic for the summer months. They are a big tourist attraction in San Diego while they migrate.

Sea mammal: Baleen Whale – Length: about 46 ft
Feeds on shellfish from seabed
Young: one calf every 2 or more years

Humpback Whale

A Humpback Whale has very long, narrow flippers and a small fin set well back on its back. It swims slower than most other whales, but is very acrobatic. It jumps clean out of the water and slaps it with its flippers as it dives back in.
Humpback Whales live in every ocean, and are often seen swimming along the coasts of North America as they migrate between polar and tropical waters. As they migrate, they sing—each group has its own song—and this probably helps to keep the group together. Their song changes as they near the Arctic, but when they begin their journey south again, they return to the song they sang before.

Sea mammal: Baleen Whale
Length: about 40 ft
Feeds on fish and plankton
Young: one calf every 2 years

Right Whale

This large, blackish whale has a big head and no fin on its back. When it blows, it produces two spouts in the shape of a "V." It was called a Right Whale by whale-hunters because it was the "right" whale to kill. It moves slowly through the water and does not sink when it is dead. At one time, herds of 100 animals would swim together, but there are now so few of them that you would be lucky to see more than twelve in a school. Although they have been protected for over fifty years, their numbers are increasing only slowly. They can be found off both the Atlantic and Pacific Coasts.

Sea mammal: Baleen Whale
Length: about 55 ft
Feeds on plankton
Young: one calf every 3–4 years

Sperm Whale

Sperm Whales are the largest toothed whales. They have very large, squarish heads and no fin on their back. It blows out an obvious, bushy plume from the tip of its head, which reaches up to 15 ft in front and to the left of it. It may blow up to twenty times before diving, and can then stay underwater for over an hour. It has broad, triangular tail flukes, which it often throws high in the air as it starts its dive. Sperm Whales can be seen off both the Atlantic and Pacific Coasts of North America. They prefer warmer seas, although some large males do migrate to polar seas in summer. Sperm whales usually live in groups of up to twenty or thirty animals. They are slow swimmers compared with other whales, and are still hunted for their oil and ambergris (a substance used in the manufacture of some perfumes).

Sea mammal: Toothed Whale
Length: about 49 ft
Feeds almost entirely on squid
Young: usually one calf about every 4 years

Killer Whale

Probably the first sign of a Killer Whale would be its large dorsal fin slicing through the water (this triangular fin can be up to 6 ft high). You can tell this whale from a shark by its large size and black and white markings. Killer Whales often swim in packs of between five and twenty-five animals, and attack young Fin Whales and even whales much larger than themselves.
It is sometimes called a Sea Wolf. Killer Whales are found in all oceans.

Sea mammal: Toothed Whale
Length: about 31 ft
Feeds mainly on fish and squid, but also on seals, sea lions, sea birds, penguins, and other whales
Young: one calf every 2–3 years

Narwhal

Narwhals are easy to identify by the long tusk that sticks out from the front of its blunt head. The tusk, which is up to 10 ft long and twists in a spiral, is used for fighting. They are closely related to White Whales, but their upper skin is heavily dappled with dark gray. Like the White Whale, Narwhals are found only along the cold Arctic Coast.

Sea mammal: Toothed Whale
Length: about 12 ft
Feeds on fish, squid, and shellfish
Young: one calf every 3–4 years

White Whale

White whales are relatively small and pure, milky white. The young are dark gray, and become white as they mature. White whales usually live in schools of between five and thirty animals, but sometimes several thousand group together. They do not move outside the cold waters of the Arctic and North Atlantic, although occasionally they have been seen as far south as Cape Cod. Although commercial whaling has stopped, White Whales are still hunted by the Inuit people.

Sea mammal: Toothed Whale
Length: about 15 ft
Feeds on fish and shellfish mostly from seabed
Young: one calf every 3–4 years

Find Out Some More

Useful Organizations

In addition to the national groups listed below, there are hundreds of natural history associations. Check with your teacher, or with your nearest natural history museum, wildlife refuge, or local public library for information on them.

Bat Conservation International is interested in everything to do with bats and their preservation. Write to: Bat Conservation International, P.O. Box 162603, Austin, Texas 78716–2603.

The **American Cetacean Society** is the best group to contact if you are interested in whales and dolphins. Write to: American Cetacean Society, P.O. Box 2639, San Pedro, California 90731.

If you are interested in wolves and in the process of reintroducing them into parts of the U.S., then contact the **Wolf Fund**. Write to: Wolf Fund, P.O. Box 471, Moose, Wyoming 83012.

The **American Society of Mammalogists** accepts professional zoologists and serious amateurs as members. Write to: American Society of Mammalogists, Department of Zoology, 501 Widtsoe Building, Provo, Utah 84602.

Many of the preserves owned by the **Nature Conservancy** and its chapters, conserve unique and threatened habitats for mammals. Write to: Nature Conservancy, Suite 800, 1800 North Kent Street, Arlington, Virginia 22209.

For a complete listing of **National Wildlife Refuges**, write to: Division of National Wildlife Refuges, Fish & Wildlife Department, Room 2343, Washington DC 20240.

Wetlands for Wildlife campaign especially for the conservation of wetlands across the U.S. Write to: Wetlands for Wildlife, 39710 Mary Lane, Oconomowoc, Wisconsin, 53066.

In Canada, the **Canadian Nature Foundation** is a good starting point. Write to: Canadian Nature Foundation, 453 Sussex Drive, Ottawa, Ontario K1N 6Z4.

Places To Visit

There are hundreds of preserves and refuges in every state—check with your teacher, or with your nearest natural history museum, wildlife refuge, or local public library for information on them. The following places are particularly worth a visit:

Baxter State Park, Millinocket, Maine: A huge area of wilderness around Mount Katahdin, Baxter is accessible by car, and is home to deer, coyote, black bear, lynx, snowshoe hars, fisher, and other mammals. Moose are very easy to see, especially feeding in ponds and lakes.

Great Smoky Mountains National Park, Tennessee–North Carolina: White-tailed deer and black bears are common, and endangered red wolves have been reintroduced. Smaller mammals include eastern chipmunks, southern flying squirrels, foxes, bobcats, and boars.

Big Bend National Park, Texas: This enormous area of the Chichuahuan Desert holds many mammals, although most only come out at night, and are hard to see. There are mountain lions, armadillos, kangaroo rats, black-tailed jack rabbits, pig-like peccaries, and mule deer.

Yellowstone National Park, Wyoming: The nation's oldest national park is one of the best for viewing Rocky Mountain mammals, including grizzly bears, elk, mule deer, bison, moose, pine martens, and coyotes.

National Bison Range, Moiese, Montana: Home to a large herd of wild bison, the refuge also holds mule and white-tailed deer, bighorn sheep, mountain goats, pronghorn, elk, badger, coyote, and other mammals.

Channel Islands National Park, Santa Barbara, California: A chain of islands off the California coast, the Channels attract large numbers of harbor seals, California sea lions, and more than 10,000 gigantic elephant seals. In winter, gray whales feed in the waters around the islands.

Index & Glossary

To find the name of a mammal in this index, search under its main name. So, to look up Gray Squirrel; look under Squirrel, not under Gray.

A

accident survey, 30
antlers, deer, 48
Armadillo, Nine-banded, 40
Antelope, 35

B

Badger, 12, 42–43
baleen plates some *whales* have these instead of teeth. They use them to sieve the water for tiny shrimps and *plankton*, 7, 46
bat, the only type of *mammal* that can fly 6, 10, 20–21, 56
Bat, Big Brown, 10
Bat, Brazilian Free-tailed, 11
Bat, Ghost-faced, 45
Bat, Red, 24
Bat, Sanborn's Long-nosed, 45
Bat, Silver-haired, 24
Bat, Spotted, 45
Bat, Townsend's Big-eared, 25
   See also Myotis, Pipistrelle
bat box, how to make, 21

bat detectors, 21
Bear, Black, 53
Bear, Grizzly, 53
Bear, Polar, 58
Beaver, 63
Beaver, Mountain, 25
Bison, 34
Bobcat, 15

C

camouflage anything that hides something or changes its appearance so that it is not easily seen, 6
Caribou, 59
casting footprints, 49
carnivore any animal that eats meat, 7

Chipmunk, Eastern, 17
Chipmunks, Western, 17
Coyote, 14
Coypu, **see** Nutria
cud, chewing the, 7

D

Deer, Mule, 11
Deer, White-tailed, 11
desert a dry, barren, sandy area where only about half the ground has any plant cover; found mostly in the Southwest of the U.S., 44
dolphin, a type of *mammal* that lives in the sea and never comes ashore 7, 46, 49

Dolphin, Bottle-nosed, 73
Dolphin, Common, 73
Dolphin, Pacific White-sided, 73
droppings, 20, 42, 49

E

echo location the way that a *bat* uses very high pitched sounds to find its food and stop it hitting things in the dark, 21, 74
Elk, 56

F

Ferret, Black-footed, 33
Fisher, 27
flippers, 7
footprints, 49
Fox, Arctic, 58
Fox, Gray, 13
Fox, Red, 13
Fox, Swift, 33

G

gland a small organ that controls certain functions of the body. Some produce milk, others scent or sweat, 6
Goat, Mountain, 56
Gopher, Plains Pocket, 39
Gopher, Southeastern Pocket, 39
Gopher, Western Pocket, 39
Gophers, Eastern Pocket, 39

Useful books

Peterson First Guide: Mammals, Peter Alden (Houghton Mifflin Co.). A simplified guide to the more common North American mammals.
Black Bear, Daniel Cox (Chronicle Books). Color photos of a year in the life of wild black bears.
World of ...., Charles Mohr (Lippincot). There are many books in the *World* of series, including bat, beaver, opossum, wolf, bobcat, squirrel, and deer.
America's Neighborhood Bats, Merlin Tuttle (University of Texas Press). A helpful guide to identifying any bat you may find.
Wild Animals of North America (National Geographic Society). A comprehensive guide to the animals of North America.
Guide to Animal Tracking & Behavior, Donald & Lilian Stokes. (Little, Brown & Co.). A useful guide, which tells you about the footprints, toothmarks, and droppings of many mammals.

Index & Glossary

Ground Squirrel, Golden-mantled, 28
Ground Squirrel, Richardson's, 38
Ground Squirrel, Thirteen-lined, 37

H
habitat a particular type of countryside, 5
Hare, Snowshoe, 29
hibernate a way of surviving the winter's cold by sleeping through it, 10

I
insectivore any animal that eats insects and other *invertebrates*, 7
invertebrate any animal that does not have an internal backbone. They include everything from *plankton* and worms to insects and lobsters

J
Jack Rabbit, Antelope, 47
Jack Rabbit, White-tailed, 38

K
Killer Whale, 77

L
Lemming, Southern Bog, 40
litter family of young animals born together, 4
Lion, Mountain, 15
Lynx, 26

M
mammal the newest addition to the animal kingdom. Almost all species have warm blood and give birth to live young who drink their mother's milk, 4–7
Manatee, 69
map, how to read a, 30–31
Marmot, Hoary, 55
Marmot, Yellow-bellied, 55
Marten, Pine, 27
mice, homes for harvest, 64–65
Mink, 61
Mole, Eastern, 16
Mole, Shrew, 28
Mole, Star-nosed, 17
Moose, 24
Mouse, Deer, 19
Mouse, Golden, 18
Mouse, Harvest, 41
Mouse, House, 19
Mouse, Meadow Jumping, 36
Mouse, Northern Grasshopper, 46
Muskrat, 62
Mustang, 35
Myotis, Little Brown, 10

N
Narwhal, 77
Nutria, 63

O
Opossum, Virginia, 25

Orca, **see** Killer Whale
Otter, River, 61
Otter, Sea, 68
otters, signs of, 42
owl pellets, rodent bones in, 65
Ox, Musk, 59

P
Peccary, Collared, 47
Pika, 54
Pipistrelle, Eastern, 10
plankton tiny *invertebrates* that live in water. Some *whales* feed on nothing else, 7, 46
Porcupine, 29
Porpoise, Harbor, 72
prairie the grasslands of central North America stretching from the Appalachians to the Rockies, 32
Prairie Dog, Black-tailed, 37
Pronghorn, 35

R
Rabbit, Eastern Cottontail, 18
Rabbit, Nuttall's Cottontail, 54
Rabbit, Pygmy, 46
Rabbit, Swamp, 62
Racoon, 14
Rat, Black, 15
Rat, Brown, 14
Rat, Eastern Wood, 55
Rat, Hispid Cotton, 36
Rat, Marsh Rice, 61
Ringtail, 52
rodent a type of *mammal* that has large front teeth for gnawing. These teeth never stop growing, 7, 68–69
roost the place where a bat spends its time sleeping or *hibernating*, 10, 20–21
runways, 64

S
savanna grassland with only a few trees and bushes and which has limited rainfall, 32
Sea Lion, Californian, 68
Sea Lion, Northern, 68
seal a type of *mammal* that mostly lives in the sea, but comes ashore to breed and to give birth to their young, 7, 44–5
Seal, Harbor, 71
Seal, Harp, 70
Seal, Hooded, 70
Seal, Northern Elephant, 71
Seal, Northern Fur, 69
Seal, Ribbon, 70
Seal, Ringed, 71
Sheep, Barbary, 57
Sheep, Bighorn, 57
Shrew, Desert, 46
Shrew, Pygmy, 16
Shrew, Short-tailed, 41
Shrew, Water, 62
Skunk, Hog-nosed, 52
Skunk, Spotted, 36
Skunk, Striped, 17
Squirrel, Fox, 29
Squirrel, Gray, 18
Squirrel, Red, 28

Squirrel, Southern Flying, 16

Squirrel, White-tailed Antelope , 47

T

tooth marks, 48, 64

tracks, 43

tragus the flap of skin of a *bat* that protects the entrance to its ear. It is an important identification point,10

tundra the stretch of land between the conifer

forests and the Arctic snows, where it is too cold for trees to grow, 64–67

U

ungulate a type of *mammal* with hooves and several stomach compartments to help it digest the plants that it eats 7

V

velvet a furry skin that covers a deer's antlers

while a new set is growing, 50

Vole, Field, 41

Vole, Sagebrush, 54

Vole, Southern Red-backed, 28

W

Walrus, 69

Weasel, Least, 33

Weasel, Long-tailed, 12

Weasel, Short-tailed, 12

whale a type of *mammal* that lives in the sea and never comes

ashore 7, 46–48

Whale, Blue, 74

Whale, Fin, 74

Whale, Gray, 75

Whale, Humpbacked, 75

Whale, Minke, 75

Whale, Right, 76

Whale, Short-finned Pilot, 72

Whale, Sperm, 76

Whale, White, 77

Wolf, Gray, 26

Wolverine, 52

Woodchuck, 19

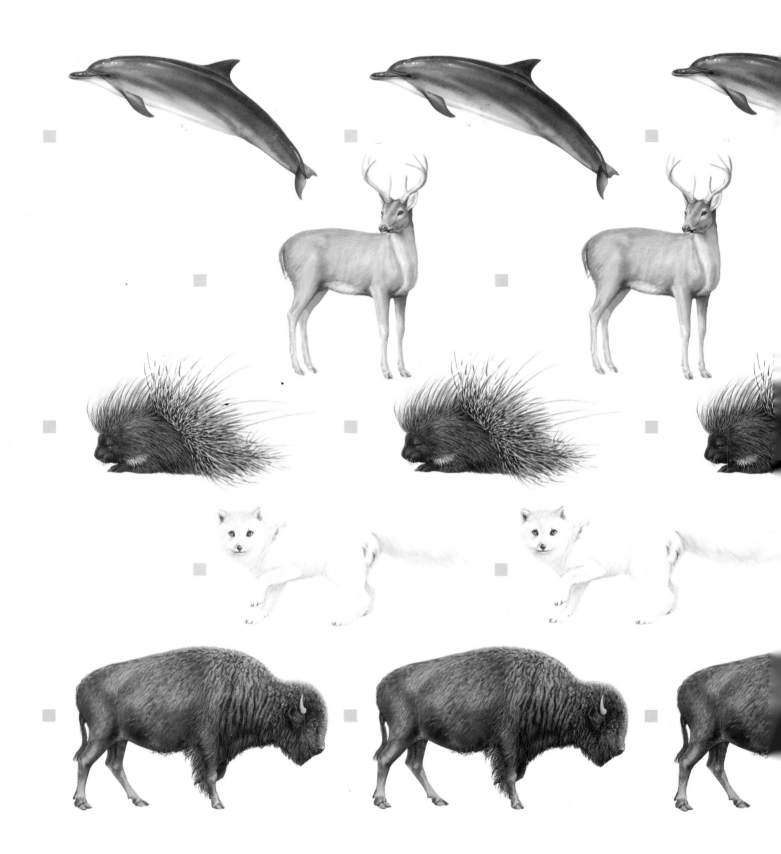